C000245746

GT YARMOUTH
AT WAR

**Colin Tooke and
David Scarles**

CONTENTS

Boats on patrol with a sentry on duty at a landing stage beneath a bridge, somewhere in Broadland. Photo Imperial War Museum

© 1989 Colin Tooke and David Scarles
Printed by Printing Services (Norwich) Ltd
Designed by Top Floor Design
Typesetting by PTPS, Norwich
First published 1989
ISBN 0 946148 41 4

FOREWORD

During the Second World War the East Coast town of Great Yarmouth suffered more bombing from the Luftwaffe than other coastal towns. The official record of these raids was published shortly after the war as 'Front Line Town' by the Chief Constable, Charles Box. His record of a town at war was unequalled by any other record of a town or city in England.

In 1970 David Scarles embarked upon a project to record the war years in greater detail and appealed in the local press for information, an appeal which was answered by Miss Rosa Bull who revealed, for the first time, a unique collection of diaries and newspaper cuttings connected with the war years. From this information David Scarles was able to put together a record of the raids as they affected Yarmouth, adding material gathered from official archives both in this country and in Germany. This work was eventually deposited in the Great Yarmouth Reference Library where for the past 20 years it has been used by researchers and students.

Now for the first time this story of a town at war is published to mark the fiftieth anniversary of the start of the war and as a tribute to those who lived through those dark years.

Miss Bull's comprehensive records logged every Alert and Raid with details of buildings damaged or destroyed, a record that she had to keep to herself for many years due to Government restrictions on such information.

I have edited David Scarles manuscript and added more information of a general nature to try and complete the picture of the town during those years and I express sincere thanks to Miss Bull, now aged 91, for her permission to include her records in this book.

I also thank the staff of the Yarmouth Reference Library who have been very helpful to David and myself during this project and to Geoff Taylor who first brought to my notice the manuscript. My good friend Ted Goate has helped with the final draft of the book for which I am also grateful.

The detail of the Naval bases has been taken from Great Yarmouth — History,Herrings and Holidays by Charles Lewis and the information concerning the Home Guard was provided by Neil Storey and I thank both these authors for letting me use their material.

Illustrations have been gathered together from many sources including the Imperial War Museum, Great Yarmouth Reference Library, Memory Lane Studios, Great Yarmouth and the collection of Percy Trett. The co-operation of the owners and custodians of these collections is acknowledged with thanks.

I have already mentioned Miss Bull but if it had not been for her original diaries this book would not have been possible.

Colin S Tooke
Caister-on-Sea
1989

The Broads Flotilla, Norfolk Division 2nd Corps, on patrol somewhere in Broadland. Photo Imperial War Museum

Great Yarmouth
Fischereihafen

Geheim
GB 458c

Kriegsaufnahme
416 R 062

Längegrdw Greenwich 1°44'   Breite 52°35'55"(Blattmitte)
Mißweisung 9°55'(Mitte 1939)

1.63360 B Nr 67
1.100000 B/Nr 10

Nachtrage
9 4 39

GREAT
YARMOUTH

SOUTHTOWN

(A)**Fischereihafen** GB 458c
1) 6 Lagerhallen   etwa 22800 qm
2) 2 Trockendocks   „   15000 „

Weitere Anlagen

5) 2 Sackbahnhöfe
6) 2 Gaswerke   etwa 17000 qm

(B) **Getreidemühlen** GB 5617c
3) 2 Getreidemühlen   etwa 8000 qm
4) Getreidesilo   „   1900 „

7) Kraftwerk   „   8000 qm
8) Säge-u.Holzverarbeitos-
   werk (für Verpackung) 7200 „
                        bebaute Fläche etwa: 79900 qm

The main target areas such as Gas Works, Southtown and Beach Railway
Stations and various Maltings are also indicated.

GREAT YARMOUTH AT WAR

PREPARING FOR WAR

With the onset of the Second World War in September 1939 the town of Great Yarmouth faced the threat of attack from two directions, an invasion from the sea and attack from the air.

In the event it was from the air that the danger, death and destruction came, between July 1940 and June 1944. The German Luftwaffe carried out more raids on Great Yarmouth than any other coastal town. During this four year period the estimated casualties were 217 persons killed and 805 injured, the evacuation of two-thirds of the towns population preventing much higher figures. A total of 237 properties were totally destroyed, 1,598 were so badly damaged they had to be demolished, 1,816 were seriously damaged but repairable and 19,818 were slightly damaged. The result of all this destruction was to change the townscape, particularly the Row area at the southern end of the old town, removing for all time the congested housing and ending a town plan that had survived since the foundation of the settlement in the 11th century.

Although this book is primarily concerned with the air attacks it may be appropriate at this point to look briefly at the defences built up in the face of threatened invasion from the sea. The town has always been regarded as one of the vulnerable points on the east coast. In the 16th century the medieval defences were strengthened as Spain set sail to conquer England, a threat that passed as the remains of the Armada sailed by. The Anglo-Dutch conflict of the mid 17th century led to the Fort at the harbour mouth being repaired and made ready to repel invading forces and almost 300 years later, following the fall of France in 1940 and the German occupation of the Low Countries, new defences were hurriedly erected at points along the east coast.

At Yarmouth three gun batteries were built; the North Battery standing at the junction of Jellicoe Road and North Drive was armed with two 6 inch ex-naval guns (these as at other batteries around the coast were at least 25 years old, having been in store since the 1920s), two searchlights and various light weapons. A second battery at the harbour mouth consisted of two 12 pounders on the end of the South Pier (one of these was moved to the Yarmouth side of the harbour entrance by mid 1941), three searchlights, one on the Gorleston side and two on the Yarmouth side, and a 40mm Bofors gun. The third battery was on Gorleston cliffs, at the Borough boundary, equipped with two 6 inch guns, two searchlights and later two 40mm Bofors and a 25 pounder field gun.

As the dangers of invasion receded and to combat the increasing air activity two batteries of heavy anti-aircraft guns were installed, one with four 4.5 inch guns at Ashby near Gorleston and another similarly armed in the middle of Gorleston golf links. Other guns were placed in strategic positions throughout the town, including one mounted on a platform beside the river on Stone Cutters Quay.

Every road leading to the sea front was barricaded with herring barrels filled with concrete; the beach was mined and obstructed with barbed wire and scaffolding. The Gorleston Cliffs were similarly defended, while a line of 20 pillboxes (several of which can still be seen today), road blocks and associated trenches formed a landward defensive line from Caister Road to the Acle New Road and continued along the line of the coastal railway to Lowestoft.

The vast waterways to the west of the town were protected by the Broads Flotilla, Norfolk Division, 2nd Corps. This flotilla of armed motor boats was operated by the Navy until 1941 when it was taken over by the Army and became part of the Army's navy. The boats patrolled the inland waterways, prepared for any enemy seaplanes that might attempt a 'landing'.

As the year 1939 progressed the country became more aware of the impending dangers and the Yarmouth summer season was cut short as people returned home during August. All entertainment centres were closed by order of the Government, the last performers at the Wellington Pier being the Vancouver Boys Band whose week run had started on August 27th. Midway through the week the show closed and by the following Monday all the seasonal entertainers had left the town.

On September 1st 4,300 mothers and children from the London area arrived at the Fishwharf in three pleasure steamers that had sailed from the Dagenham Docks. They were the first of a total of 7,500 evacuees to arrive in the town during the following three days for a short stay before being moved to the Midlands, to areas that were then regarded as safe. Yarmouth was, at this time, declared a 'neutral' area, neither to be evacuated or receive evacuees, and during the month over 50,000 people were moved from London to Norfolk and Suffolk. Many of these children stayed in Bradwell and Belton although a lot drifted back to London before they could be moved further inland.

The schools in the town closed until the necessary shelters had been built, the first to reopen being the Cobholm Infants and St Mary's RC in Albion Road in November 1939.

The herring industry ceased to operate in 1939 and by early the following year two naval bases had been established in the harbour, their role being to protect the offshore convoy routes. HMS *Miranda* operated minesweeping trawlers and the other, HMS *Midge*, operated motor torpedo boats and motor gunboats which were used for countering E-boat attacks, raiding enemy convoys off the Dutch coast and running secret agents into Holland.

Air Raid Precautions had first been considered in 1935 and in 1937 the town appointed the Town Clerk, Farra Conway OBE MA as ARP Officer. In December that year a public meeting was held to explain the objects and duties of the ARP scheme and the following year a Wardens' Committee was formed to organise groups and establish a Warden System. In the book Front Line Town, published just after the war as an official account of the ARP activities and enemy action within the town, the Chief Constable and ARP Controller Charles Box outlined the system adopted by the town when a warning was given.

The public sirens sounded the 'Alert', many of these lasting for a considerable time. To avoid stoppages in work and business, except in periods of imminent danger, an industrial alarm within the alert, locally known as the 'Crash' warning was sounded by means of steam whistles, and on the public sirens by the fitting of an attachment called the 'Cuckoo'. During the war years there were 2,046 Alerts and 1,854 Crash warnings in the town.

Upon the sounding of a warning, or in the absence of a warning, upon hostile action or gun-fire, the Wardens, both male and female, patrolled their various sectors and in the event of an incident made a rapid assessment of the situation and reported, usually by telephone, to the Report Centre that had been established at the Art School, Trafalgar Road.

At the Report Centre were based the officials able to make decisions and call for assistance such as the Medical Officer of Health, Borough Engineer, liaison officers from the Police and Fire Services, ARP Officer and representatives of the Gas, Electricity, Water and Telephone companies.

Built in 1912 and now known as the College of Art and Design this became the Civil Defence Report Centre for the duration of the war. All Warden reports were received here and the rescue efforts co-ordinated.

AIR RAID PRECAUTIONS
IMPORTANT TO EVERY HOUSEHOLDER

1 This card is issued on behalf of the A.R.P. Committee of the Borough Council. It should be carefully studied and kept and the information brought to the notice of all members of your household.

2 **KNOW YOUR WARDENS.** Your nearest Wardens' Post is

VANCOUVER AVENUE.

and is the link between you and the vital services. It is most important that you should afford every help to the Wardens attached to the Post. If possible get to know them now and ask if there is anything that you can do to help. They may be glad for you to have a bucket of sand or water standing in your garden in readiness for an emergency. If so let them know exactly where the bucket is and keep it filled. In the event of any unexploded bombs or other missiles dropping on or near your premises, the occurrence should be reported as soon as possible to the patrolling Wardens or to the Wardens' Post or to a Police Officer. Keep your Warden informed of your movements, *i.e.*, if you are going away, let them know.

3 **LIGHTS. Be very careful of your lights whether from windows or opened doors, skylights or torches.** If you go out to a shelter, be sure to turn off the lights in your house before you leave. Turn off your gas at the main if there is a raid on the Borough. If you go out in the evening, do not leave a fire in a room with unscreened windows.

4 **GAS MASKS.** If you want advice about your gas mask, go to your Wardens' Post. Make sure it is not defective in any way. If you wish to exchange or replace it, apply to A.R.P. OFFICE, TOWN HALL. Always carry your mask wherever you may be. It has been issued to you for instant readiness.

5 **PROTECTION AGAINST GAS ATTACKS.** It is emphasised again—carry your gas mask always. If you have been in contact with Gas and your **clothes** are contaminated, go home quickly or go to a friend's house, discard your clothing before going indoors, have a bath and put on clean clothing.

If your eyes are affected by gas, or if you have inhaled gas, or if any part of your body is affected by gas spray or vapour, go to one of the First Aid Posts mentioned in paragraph 6. The best way to protect yourself from gas is to stay in your shelter (if you have one) or remain indoors. If the shelter or room is not gas proof, wear your gas mask. Everybody who has no other duties to perform should adopt these precautions when gas has been used. The Wardens will endeavour to warn you of the presence of gas by using their rattles.

6 **CASUALTIES.** If you have received injuries but can walk, go to the **First Aid Post at West Norfolk and King's Lynn General Hospital**; or the **First Aid Points :—**

> **Castle Rising Road, South Wootton**
> **Old School, Gayton Road, Gaywood**
> **Old School, near Church, West Lynn.**

7 **INCENDIARY BOMBS.** Keep a look-out for these on your house or your neighbour's. Deal with them promptly either with a stirrup pump or with sand or soil. If you have none of these things at hand, call the Wardens or the nearest voluntary Fire Party or a neighbour who has a stirrup pump or other means of putting a fire out. Everyone, ordinary householders as well as owners of business premises, must learn one of the great lessons of the war. Their first protection against fire is not the brigade, it is themselves. Only by the united work of ordinary men and women, not by fire services alone, can we be saved from the enemy's worst weapon. **Fires are beacons which tell following enemy planes where to drop their HE. Bombs.**

P.T.O.

All households were informed of the nearest ARP post.

The Warden's report was taken down by the telephonist and the appropriate services were despatched, such as Rescue and First Aid parties (which were later merged), while First Aid Posts and hospitals were prepared to receive casualties. The Wardens kept the centre informed with intermediate reports and the police, fire and utility services kept their own organisations informed.

Each incident was recorded on an Operation Board. Where temporary shelter was required the Rest Centres were brought into operation and the Billeting Officer looked after cases where people needed to be rehoused.

Unexploded bombs were dealt with by the Royal Navy (responsible for the docks area) and the Army, while in the event of a gas attack there were trained Gas Identification Officers. The ARP Mortuaries were run by the Mortuary Superintendent.

Thus at the beginning of the war the ARP could call on five ambulance stations (later increased to nine) each station equipped with three ambulances, four First Aid Posts and six First Aid Party Depots, three of which were on daytime duty and three on night duty. Feeding and Rest Centres were established and by 1941 there were ten sleeping centres, mostly in Methodist Churches or Halls. (For location of these First Aid Posts etc see Appendix.)

From September 1939 until August 1941 all fire fighting was under the control of the Chief Constable and was carried out by members of the Police Force and Auxiliary Fire Service. The town was served by 14 stations and there were 350 whole and part time firemen backed up by 40 male and female telephonists.

With the introduction of the National Fire Service in August 1941 the fire services in the town became Sub Divisions 1 and 2 of Division B No.13 Fire Force.

Firewatchers, whose duty it was to watch for and report the fall of incendiary bombs, were introduced and later in the war a Fire Guard Plan was put into operation with Fire Guard Officers.

Early in 1940 a national force, known as the Local Defence Volunteers, was formed from men who, for one reason or another, were not at the time engaged in military service. In every town men wishing to help with the defence of the country enlisted at local police stations and in Great Yarmouth three Companies were formed.

No 1 Company was based at Church Road, Gorleston, No 2 Company was based at the Hospital School which was also the Group Headquarters and No 3 Company was first based at the Art School (also the ARP Report Centre) but later moved to St Peters School. In the early days the only item of uniform was a khaki arm band bearing the letters LDV, and the only weapons were ex First World War American rifles.

Two NCOs and 12 men provided a guard for the two Gas Works and the Beach Railway Station, using as transport lorries requisitioned from local coal merchants.

Members of the 2nd and 8th Great Yarmouth Scout Troops setting up a practice Report Centre as part of the towns Air Raid training in 1939. This exercise was in the old Barracks buildings at the south end of town. Photo Gordon Berry

Members of the AFS team based at Grouts Silk Factory in 1941. From Left to right: R Snowling, D Brown, D Jenkins, T Haylett, F Cox, G Brown, S Harrison. Photo R Snowling

By November 1941 military uniforms were issued to the men and the following month the Battalion HQ moved to No 6 Regent Road. Extensive training took place on Sundays and most evenings, interspersed with camps and exercises, and the Battalion became proficient in rifle shooting, stretcher bearing, first aid and signalling.

By mid 1941 the name had changed, the force being known as the Home Guard, and a more mobile role, that of coastal patrol, was adopted. Several German airmen were captured by the various platoons stationed along the coastal section which stretched northwards to Sea Palling.

With these services in operation the town prepared itself to receive the worst from the Luftwaffe. Although most damage was done by full scale attacks made on specific targets such as the port facilities and gas works, the town also suffered damage from planes en route for the Midlands, dropping their bombs as they entered or left the country over this area, while other planes, caught inland by RAF fighters, jettisoned their bombs over the first likely target as they were chased out to sea. Mine-laying aircraft, either by accident or design, dropped their mines on coastal targets instead of in the sea and in the early years of the war reconnaissance planes, which also carried bombs, singled out Yarmouth as their target.

The main air attacks on England were carried out by squadrons of Heinkel 111 and Junkers 88 aircraft based in France, Holland and Belgium and the following account is by a Luftwaffe officer concerning the bombing of Yarmouth.

"...After very few attacks during daylight we changed our attacks to very early in the evening, the reason being the first class organised air defence and brilliant and brave defence of the English fighter squadrons. These night attacks used to be single flights at short term intervals, at different heights on the scale of an exact flight plan. Because of strong air defence, at attack points like Yarmouth, we used to fly in from the sea and enter as late as possible the air defence corridor. Normally the approach was guided by a radio beam on the point of attack. The loss of aircraft

The AFS Team grouped around their fire engine at the Silk Factory. Photo R Snowling

Among the many buildings camouflaged against air attack was Smiths Crisp Factory on Caister Road. Photo P Trett

and men during the attacks on England increased with each attack."

The defence of East Anglia was, at the beginning of the war, covered by airfields at Duxford and Debden but as hostilities increased it became apparent that additional airfields were required. A bomber station had been commenced at Coltishall in 1939 but in May 1940 its role was changed to that of a fighter station and it was from here the RAF squadrons flew to defend Yarmouth and the coastal area. 66 Squadron was based there to guard coastal shipping and in June 1940 242 Squadron arrived, under the command of Squadron Leader D R S Bader. This squadron was replaced later in the year by 72 Squadron but the Hurricanes of 257 Squadron, which arrived in December 1940, came to be looked on as Coltishall's own. They stayed for 11 months. By the end of 1940 the station had claimed 83 enemy aircraft shot down. Many other squadrons were based at Coltishall during the war period, flying a variety of planes, although the Spitfires and Beaufighters remained the main weapons in the air defence of the region.

The bombs used by the Luftwaffe were of three main types. The High Explosive Bomb, of which 997 were dropped, contained from 50 to 500 kilograms of explosive (later increased to 2500 kilos), Incendiary

bombs weighing 21 pounds and 18 inches long were dropped in containers of various sizes (the average being 72 bombs to a crate) and Parachute Mines, always dropped in pairs.

It was recorded that in total 9060 Incendiary bombs were dropped. Later versions were the Phosphorus bomb, with ten dropped in 1942, and Firepot Incendiaries. The Mines, of which ten were dropped, were known as the Parachute Type and G Type and could cause considerable damage as they exploded above ground, the blast spreading outwards at ground level.

War had been declared at 11am on Sunday September 3rd 1939 and the following day the first Air Raid Alert was sounded, at 2.45am. After a peaceful 90 minutes the All Clear was given but two days later another Alert was sounded at 6.45am. Again there was no sight of the enemy and the All Clear was given 30 minutes later. These two Alerts, coming so soon after the hostilities had been announced brought home to the town the seriousness of the situation although many people still believed the war would be over by Christmas.

The remainder of that year and the first few months of 1940 were known as the 'twilight war' or 'phoney war' and to many it seemed an anti-climax after all the preparation. The 'black out', rationing and general austerity however were constant reminders that a war was in progress.

1940 – THE BOMBING STARTS

The first few months of 1940 saw a continuation of the 'phoney war'. There was even some consideration given to a Summer Holiday Season, plans for which were not abandoned until May. The fishwharf area came under naval occupation when the two bases were established and the town purchased 600 Anderson shelters, larger public shelters being erected in Southtown, Cobholm and the Row areas.

The German occupation of the Low Countries prompted the Ministry of Health to issue orders to evacuate children from many coastal towns and on Sunday June 2nd 47,000 children, from 18 East Coast towns, were evacuated in 97 special trains.

In Yarmouth only 40% of the school population registered for evacuation, described in official terms as disappointing. About three-quarters of the Grammar School's 229 boys were evacuated to Retford but many soon began to return to the town, despite official pleas to parents not to bring their children back.

Adult evacuation followed soon after and the town's pre-war population of 54,000 was eventually reduced as about 34,000 people, considered non-essential workers, and their families, were moved to inland areas. This policy of evacuation was carried out in many coastal towns which then became 'restricted areas', people only being allowed into the area if they lived there or had a special pass.

On August 30th the King, on a tour of East Anglia, visited the town arriving by train to inspect the defences and meet minesweeper crews. A detachment of Newfoundland troops, stationed near the town, and locally based WRENS were also inspected by the Royal visitor.

The Chief Warden assumed responsibility for all Wardens, a job previously delegated to the ARP Officer, and an Assistant to the Chief Warden was appointed.

As the year progressed the threat of an invasion receded but the air attacks increased. This was to be the year of the Battle of Britain.

Parents wave goodbye to the children leaving Vauxhall Station on the evacuation train, Sunday June 2nd 1940. On this Sunday over 47,000 children were evacuated from 18 East Coast towns in 97 special trains. Photo Imperial War Museum

COUNTY BOROUGH OF GREAT YARMOUTH
EDUCATION COMMITTEE.

GOVERNMENT EVACUATION SCHEME.

28th May, 1940.

Dear Sir, Madam,

The Government have decided that the school children of Great Yarmouth shall be evacuated to places of safety in the Midlands or in Wales. Exact information concerning destinations will not be available until Saturday next, 1st June.

The Government strongly urge that every parent shall take advantage of the evacuation scheme now being prepared. You are free to make up your mind. **BUT YOU MUST MAKE UP YOUR MIND AT ONCE.** It is your duty to do so for the sake of your children. The Authorities cannot make their plans at all if they do not know the number for whom they must provide.

Parents who desire their children to be evacuated should complete the form of consent which will be issued by the Head Teacher. **THIS FORM MUST BE RETURNED TO THE SCHOOL BY 9 O'CLOCK ON WEDNESDAY MORNING, 29th MAY.**

It is expected that the parties will leave Great Yarmouth by train on Sunday, 2nd June, and will be accompanied by their teachers.

If you want any help, or there is anything you do not understand, go to your child's school where you will get full information of the arrangements.

Yours faithfully,

G. J. WROUGHTON,

Clerk to the Committee.

Education Offices,
  28, South Quay,
    Great Yarmouth.

The official letter to parents informing them of the evacuation proposals in May 1940.   *Reproduced by permission of the Norfolk Museum Service.*

JULY 11th

6.30am Four killed, three injured.

This first raid on Great Yarmouth was carried out by a Dornier 17Z on a weather reconnaissance flight. No air-raid siren was sounded as the plane, flying out of low cloud over the sea, dropped its bombs on the junction of Gordon Road and Wolseley Road, Southtown, with more falling on the nearby marshes. An eye-witness said "After the bombs were dropped two Spitfires appeared and they played about like gnats above and below the Germans, their guns squirting intermittently. They eventually drove the plane into the clouds."

The two Spitfires were from 66 Squadron based at Coltishall and the enemy plane was eventually shot down near Cromer.

The bombs, which were of the whistling type and quite small, fell on houses in Gordon Road, two receiving direct hits. A young man, in bed in a house nearby, had a remarkable escape when his bedroom floor collapsed and his bed fell into the kitchen below. He emerged shaken but unhurt. Three men walking along the road were machine-gunned and narrowly escaped injury by taking cover in a nearby passage.

Requests for help were made to the Report Centre at 6.38am. A first-aid party was sent from the Cobholm post to attend the wounded and at 6.40am an ambulance was summoned from Watson's garage. A rescue squad of six men was on the scene some 40 minutes later. This was the first time the ARP services had been called into action and the organisation proved itself very capable and efficient.

Prior to this first raid there had been enemy activity in the vicinity of the town on July 9th and 10th but no bombs had been dropped. A Heinkel 111, based in Belgium and a Dornier 17Z, also based in Belgium, were shot down.

JULY 24th

6.18pm No casualties.

13 days after the first raid another Dornier 17Z bombed the town in early evening, dropping six high-explosive bombs.

Two fell in the Queens Road area while the remainder fell across the harbour mouth. At 6.25pm St James First Aid Post advised the Report Centre that in the garden of 32 Queens Road there was a large crater in which lay an unexploded bomb. The Report Centre requested a unit from Norwich to attend to make the bomb safe.

The actual message sent read:

TIME 1830   NORWICH 3664
No 8 BOMB DISPOSAL SECTION
Object dropped presumed UXHE bomb at 32 Queens Road

The Yarmouth Mercury of 13th July 1940 reported the first air raid on the town. Note that no information that could locate the target of the raid was given, a security procedure that was enforced on all such reporting throughout the war years.

also Camden Road near Royal Naval Hospital. Please report at Art School Nelson Road.

End of message.

The other bomb had damaged a water main and the Nelson Gardens AFS attended, the water supply being restored by 7.15pm.

On July 23rd a Junkers 88 was shot down south east of the town by a Hurricane from 242 Squadron based at Coltishall.

AUGUST 20th

5.40pm No casualties.

Another Dornier 17Z dropped 20 high-explosive bombs and ten incendiaries in the area of High Road and Beccles Road, Gorleston and Common and Boundary

Roads, Southtown, at tea-time. High Road and Ferry Hill became impassable to traffic as a result of a crater and a burst water main. Two houses were hit and an electricity sub-station demolished at the bottom of the ferry steps. In Beccles Road electricity cables were brought down and the AFS unit from Yareside Works dealt with fires which damaged nine houses.

On the same day another Dornier 17Z attacked a shipping convoy off Aldeburgh and an Me 110D was shot down near Yarmouth.

AUGUST 24th

8.05am One killed, five injured.

The Battle of Britain was reaching its climax and there was considerable air activity over the whole country towards the end of August. Heavy cloud for four days had prevented the Luftwaffe flying any sorties but on the morning of the 24th the sun broke through and the radar picked up an almost continuous stream of bombers and fighters joining together over Calais. This attack on the town was the beginning of heavy and sustained raids on sector stations and fighter airfields in the south east of Great Britain.

A total of 20 high-explosive bombs was dropped in a line, approximately 40 yards apart, over an area of Gorleston stretching from Bells Marsh Road to Beach Road. In Bells Marsh Road 138 was demolished as was the British Legion Club in Pier Walk. 8 Beach Road was demolished and 106 and 107 Upper Cliff Road damaged.

The only fatality was an elderly lady, Mrs Bush, killed just after she had left 5 Beach Road, a shop which was destroyed by a direct hit. The owner of the shop and his wife were buried under the ruins but were eventually released uninjured. Many people had remarkable escapes during this raid.

An eye-witness described the scene as follows. "A long trail of damage followed a straight line across an area of houses and cottages that at this time of the year are usually overflowing with summer visitors. Although at first sight it seemed strange that all this damage was accompanied by so little loss of life this puzzling feature was resolved by reflecting that the occupiers of many of the damaged houses had moved elsewhere. In one road gaped a crater that revealed sewers, gas and electricity mains. A hundred yards away in the next street a bomb dug a crater in the garden into which the front of two houses collapsed... A garden hut often used as a summer house was demolished when a large lump of concrete fell through the roof."

Damage to public services was great but by 6.02pm the water mains were 60% repaired, as were 75% of the telephones in the area. Many roads were blocked, some not to be reopened for many days. Beach Road reopened four days later but Bells Marsh Road remained closed until September 6th.

The remains of the British Legion Club, Pier Walk, Gorleston, following the raid on August 24th 1940. Photo Great Yarmouth Library

The following communique was issued at 12.30pm by the Air Ministry and Ministry of Home Security.

"Reports of this mornings activities received up to 11am show that enemy aircraft dropped bombs on a town on the coast where damage was done to some houses and a small number of casualties was caused."

These official communiques, careful not to reveal the location of the bombing, did not reflect on the real damage and destruction caused or the upheaval in the lives of the ordinary citizen of the area.

SEPTEMBER 10th

11.30am Two killed, five injured.

This raid was one of several carried out by Dornier bombers over East Anglia just before mid-day. Norwich also received some damage, but due to the scattered nature of the attack and the thick cloud there was no reaction from the Coltishall fighters.

Number 40 Harbord Crescent suffered a direct hit, houses on either side being badly damaged, at 11.30am on September 10th 1940. Photo Great Yarmouth Library

Four bombs were dropped at the south end of the town, one falling on open ground, one on the scenic railway at the Pleasure Beach, and a third in a yard opposite the AFS station, the blast throwing two firemen out of their bunks. The fourth bomb scored a direct hit on 40 Harbord Crescent. The house was empty but the houses either side were completely wrecked and in one of these a young woman was killed. The second fatality of this raid was a lady in the other wrecked house, brought out of the ruins with her potato peeling knife still in her hand.

As usual there were remarkable escapes. The woman next door had started to shepherd her family into the Anderson shelter when the raid had begun only to be blown in herself by the blast, landing on the bed. A young boy chopping wood in the back yard of the house on the other side of the road had a lucky escape from the flying debris and his sister was knocked unconscious when her father grabbed her and threw her into the cupboard under the stairs. Washing from the gardens in Harbord Crescent was deposited on the scenic railway by the blast.

Four other bombs dropped in this raid did not explode and were dealt with by the Bomb Disposal Unit,

one at the back of Nelson's Monument, damaging a Naval Maintenance store and water main, one on a fish curing works and two on houses at the southern end of Harbord Crescent.

SEPTEMBER 14th

3.45pm 12 injured.

It is reasonable to assume that this raid was also carried out by a Dornier 17Z. Approaching the town from the west it dropped a bomb on the Nelson Gardens, Marine Parade whilst a game of bowls was in progress, four players being injured by flying glass. One of the players was the groundsman who said "We saw an aeroplane coming over from the west and someone said, 'That's a jerry!' Then there was a whistle that sent us down on our faces, and almost immediately a bomb came down and exploded ten yards away."

A second bomb fell 50 yards away, wrecking a beach shelter, and another landed on the grass field in front of the Royal Naval Hospital, failing to explode. Another bomb which also failed to explode landed on the beach

150 yards south of the Wellington Pier, and lay between the barbed wire defences and the sea, in the centre of the mine field laid as an anti-invasion measure.

The Bomb Disposal Unit again got to work and it was exploded the following day as was the one in front of the Naval Hospital.

On the 19th of the month six high-explosive bombs fell into the sea off the Britannia Pier.

OCTOBER 5th
11.35pm No casualties.

The Dornier 17Z of 11/KG3 based at Antwerp left its base at 2140 hours and on arrival over the town circled for some time before dropping its bombs in the area of Beaconsfield Recreation Ground and Sandown Road, one bomb completely wrecking the dressing rooms on the Recreation Ground. The Parks Superintendent's house at 1 Sandown Road and 61 and 65 Wellesley Road were all damaged as were nearby Corporation greenhouses.

The other bomb fell near the railway line about 600 yards from Beach Station causing slight damage to the track. A third bomb fell near the main signal box but failed to explode.

OCTOBER 11th
Alert 8.57pm to 9.03pm One killed.

Again bombs fell in the North Drive area. 12 high-explosive bombs were dropped by a lone raider, one damaging the house of Dr Mickie on the corner of Marine Parade and Salisbury Road and the public lavatory on the opposite side of the Parade.

Another bomb landed in the Waterways and another in the garden of 7 Marine Crescent, causing damage to both 7 and 8.

A dance was in progress at the Royal Aquarium, in aid of the local Spitfire Fund, and this was temporarily halted when a bomb exploded on the beach, breaking windows. The band soon carried on, as did the dancers.

After the raid two unexploded bombs were found, one at the junction of Marine Parade and Beaconsfield Road and the other on the North beach near an anti-aircraft gun post.

Although not part of the raids on Yarmouth it is interesting to note the Luftwaffe losses over the next few days.

The crater made by a 900lb armour piercing bomb which destroyed the Pavilion on the Beaconsfield Recreation Ground on October 5th 1940. Photo Great Yarmouth Library

The damaged Pavilion on the Recreation Ground after the late morning raid on October 5th 1940. Photo Great Yarmouth Library

On October 14th a Dornier 17Z based in Holland was shot down and on October 25th an Me 110 based in France was shot down 15 miles north east of Yarmouth by a Spitfire of 72 Squadron.

Two days later at Saltfleet a Heinkel 111 was shot down by a Hurricane and on the same day a Dornier 17Z, whose target was Martlesham, was also shot down by a Hurricane.

OCTOBER 31st

2.35pm Eight injured.

The Italian Air Force had joined in the war by now and there was a tendency for many eye-witnesses to describe German planes as Italian, and such was the case in this raid. Several contemporary reports state that a lone Italian plane was responsible. While this is possible the evidence leans towards a plane of the Luftwaffe.

A stick of four bombs, of the screaming type, were dropped as the plane power-dived the town. One fell on Regent Road opposite Sutton's Fish Shop, bursting a water main but not exploding, while the second was a direct hit on the Eastern Star public **house** on the corner of Union and Middle Market Roads. The third bomb fell on Nettle Hill East and the fourth scored a direct hit on Hills Marine View, on the corner of Marine Parade and Euston Road.

The Regent Road bomb caused the road to be closed until the water main was repaired and the bomb made safe, while at the Eastern Star two people were injured and the Co-op Dairy, on the opposite side of the road, was damaged. The AFS section from nearby Grouts Factory attended this incident.

The Nettle Hill bomb fell on a site where only the previous day it had been decided to build an air raid shelter. Casualties here were caused by flying glass. The worst of the four incidents was the direct hit on Hill's Marine View, where the guests had just completed luncheon. The hotel secretary was buried under rubble as the room she was in collapsed. She was rescued 30 minutes later by soldiers who had to tunnel through the wreckage to reach her. Two other people at the hotel were buried. One was a naval Captain buried under a water tank. He is reputed to have said "I have been to sea all my life and now I look like being drowned on dry land."

On November 5th a high-explosive bomb fell harmlessly on the marshes off Caister Road.

Extensive damage was caused to Hill's Marine View hotel on the corner of Euston Road and North Drive in the raid on October 31st 1940. Photo Great Yarmouth Library

NOVEMBER 10th

4.56pm Two injured.

Ground defences went into action on this Sunday afternoon when a lone raider flew the length of the town before selecting the Gas Works as his target. The bomb, of the high-explosive type, fell near the Royal Naval Hospital, striking a wall in Admiralty Road.

Two people were slightly injured and one eyewitness described how he saw the bomb leave the plane before he made a desperate race for a shelter. A little girl, hearing the whistle of the bomb, picked up her baby brother and ran to the back of the house only seconds before the front windows were blown in. A small shop caught the full force of the explosion and was wrecked. Windows were shattered and doors blown off their hinges over a wide area.

NOVEMBER 21st

8.38am One killed, three injured.

In this raid a Dornier 17Z dropped 12 high-explosive bombs in the area of Arundel, Churchill and Walpole Roads. One hit 78 Churchill Road and in Walpole Road a lady was killed when her house was destroyed by a direct hit, a woman and two children being dug out of another damaged house uninjured.

Four bombs fell in the Infirmary (Northgate Hospital) grounds, but did no damage.

Will's cigarettes produced a series of cards with advice on protection against bombing.

DECEMBER 7th

12.13pm Two injured.

The apparent objective of this raid, by a single Dornier 17Z, was the Naval Hospital, then used as a Naval Barracks. Coming in over the sea it dropped four high-explosive bombs, one hitting the yacht pond next to the Pleasure Beach. In the Gunner public house the landlord was playing darts with some customers when they heard the plane. They dived for cover as the windows were blown in. Other bombs fell near the Barrack Estate and one damaged a water main on Marine Parade.

DECEMBER 16th

3.13am No casualties.

In this raid only one bomb was dropped and this fell in the doorway of 158 King Street, failing to explode. The inhabitants of the area were evacuated for several days until the bomb was defused.

This was the last raid of the year, the town being left to a peaceful if austere Christmas, not realising what was to come in 1941.

1941 – THE RAIDS INTENSIFY

This was the worst year of the war for Great Yarmouth. Regular and frequent raids destroyed many buildings, blocked roads and killed 109 people. Over 7,000 incendiary bombs and 800 high-explosive bombs were dropped on the town.

In addition to the Anderson shelters provided the previous year the Corporation now provided Morrison (indoor) shelters. These doubled as kitchen tables and with their steel-plate tops were capable of withstanding the weight of a collapsed house. Many people now spent the night sleeping 'under the table'. More communal shelters were built during the year, some earlier ones resited and others demolished. As more people began to use these shelters on a regular basis lighting, heating and improved toilet facilities were provided.

One of the town's landmarks for many years, the Revolving Tower north of Britannia Pier, was demolished in 1941. Not only was the metal required for scrap but the tower probably gave enemy planes a splendid landmark.

The Revolving Observation Tower which had stood on a site to the north of the Britannia Pier since 1897 was demolished in 1941 for scrap metal. The tower had probably also served as a landmark for enemy planes. Photo Memory Lane Studio

There were three Royal visits to the town during 1941. In April the Duke of Gloucester made an evening visit and toured the damaged areas and the following month the Duke of Kent inspected Civil Defence workers, firemen, first-aid workers and wardens. In August the Duchess of Kent visited the naval barracks to meet members of the WRNS.

The 11th Battalion Norfolk Home Guard, 'C' Company, outside the Hospital School in the Market Place, 1941. Photo Neil Storey

JANUARY 9th

9.25pm Two injured.

The first raid of 1941 was carried out by a Dornier 17Z flying very low and slow from the west, dropping 14 high-explosive bombs.

Blackwall Reach was blocked, electricity being cut off in the area, and other bombs fell on Precasters Yard and Suttons Ice House. Tavern Lane was hit as were fish curing yards on the South Denes, the target of this raid appearing to be the harbour installations.

A message from the Report Centre at 2206 hours read:

"Have despatched LTP and crew to assist a trawler Peba, 200 yards south of Rotunda, bombed and listing heavily."

After the raider had passed over the town and flown out to sea another Dornier 17Z approached, also from the west, but was driven off by the anti-aircraft units before it could drop its bombs.

JANUARY 23rd

11.11am One injured.

Four days before this raid a Junkers 88 based in Holland had attacked the trawler *Gavahi* off Yarmouth and was shot down by the trawler's guns, crashing at Somerton.

A single Dornier 17Z appeared over the town in the late morning of the 23rd, from a southerly direction, flying low over the Market Place. It eventually dropped two bombs on Caister Road, one of which destroyed two empty cottages and the other destroyed number 66 Caister Road, injuring one occupant, Mrs Florence Wharton.

The raider was pursued by two fighters and a hail of machine-gun bullets hit the streets, at a time when the children were coming out of school. Fortunately the children scattered for cover and no one was injured.

As the plane left the town it dropped another seven high-explosive bombs but these fell harmlessly on the marshes.

JANUARY 25th

3.19pm Seven killed, 13 Injured.

At the height of Saturday afternoon shopping ten high-explosive bombs were dropped in a line extending from Sacrets in Middlegate Street, Queen Street, South Quay and across the river to Southtown. The objective of this raid was almost certainly the Naval trawlers and merchant shipping moored in the harbour and the extensive wood yards on the Gorleston side.

Several boats were damaged including HMS *Themerit*, SS *Polyanna* and HMS *Blyth*. One seaman was killed on a Norwegian boat moored at Jewsons Timber Yard. The bomb that fell on Sacrets premises failed to explode and this necessitated the evacuation of the nearby Police Station and Central Fire Station in Middlegate.

The plane was so low as it came in on its bombing run that as the first bomb hit the ground the last was seen to leave the bomb bay. The solicitors' office of Chamberlin Talbot and Bracey in Queen Street was hit. One solicitor watching from his window on the other side of the street saw his colleague's office crumble into smoke and flame as the bomb hit. A lady cleaner was killed in the office and a man standing at the door of his shop was blown inside by the blast from a bomb which fell on the opposite side of the road, but he was unhurt except for a blow on the head from a falling bottle.

Other property was damaged in Queen Street and Rows 70, 104, 129 and 132. A soldier, on leave from the 8th Battalion Royal Norfolks, was killed. Campling's Laundry, Crabtrees' Yard and a Newspaper Office were all damaged in this raid. A German communique issued in the evening said:

"On the British East Coast two merchant ships as well as installations of Military importance at a Harbour were bombed."

Only an hour before this raid two high-explosive bombs were dropped into the sea off the Harbour's Mouth.

FEBRUARY 1st

8.02am No casualties.

Just after breakfast time an enemy plane with all its navigation lights on dropped 12 high-explosive bombs on allotments off Boundary Road, Southtown. Damage was caused to the roof of the Slipper Factory and windows in nearby houses were blown in. Boundary Road was closed for some time. The target of this raid was probably the railway line.

The only casualties were five rabbits on the allotments.

FEBRUARY 1st

12.21pm Three killed, nine injured.

In this second raid of the day a Dornier 17Z, flying in from the north, dropped 12 high-explosive bombs in a low level attack on an area stretching from Kitchener Road to Middle Market Road.

The damage on the east side of the Silk Mill, February 1st 1941. Photo Gordon Berry

One bomb hit the South Mill of Grout's Silk Factory and started a fire. The raider was so low that bombs ricocheted from the roadway, penetrating the upper storeys of premises close by. One bounced off houses until it eventually struck Dyson's Glass Store on the corner of Middle and North Market Roads. One man was killed and another saved by a wall inside the

The west side of Grouts Silk Mill, February 1st 1941. Photo Gordon Berry

An aerial view of Grouts Silk Factory taken in 1934. The two five storey buildings in the centre of the picture, the Silk Throwing Mills, were severely damaged in a raid on February 1st 1941 and later demolished. Photo Gordon Berry

glass store while two workmen outside escaped by diving under their barrow, which was covered by flying debris.

At Grout's Factory the firemen fought for two hours to control the blaze. The watchman was killed but heavy casualties were avoided as the workers had left the factory less than half an hour before the raid.

Bombs fell on numbers 1 and 6 Kitchener Road, Maygrove and Belvidere Road. A child was injured in the street and a milkman killed while on his delivery round. An unexploded bomb was later found in Leaches Warehouse in Manby Road.

The following day a Junkers 88 was shot down off Yarmouth by a plane fron 22 Squadron and two days later a Dornier 17Z was shot down 5 miles south east of the town.

FEBRUARY 5th

10pm Four killed, 23 injured.

Ten high-explosive bombs dropped by a raider flying north to south across the town fell in a line from Palgrave Road to the Regal Cinema. At the cinema the film *The Doctor Takes a Wife*, starring Lorretta Young was just coming to the end when a bomb burst through the roof, just in front of the stage, and exploded. There was no panic as great lumps of masonry fell into the cinema and surprisingly there were no serious casualties. A small fire was dealt with a stirrup pump.

The Warden Post at Electric House, almost next door to the cinema, relayed the following to the Report Centre at 2200 hours. "Bombs dropped on Regal, light shining from roof." A message from the Police, one minute later said "Fire at Regal." Messages were sent to the First Aid Post at the North Mission, Northgate Street and the Ambulance Station at Kings Garage to proceed to the Regal and 19 minutes later the fire was reported under control. By 2225 hours the First Aid Party had returned to their post and ten minutes later the ambulance returned to its post, an example of the efficient working of the Report Centre.

Another bomb had hit Fish Street, (between Theatre Plain and Market Gates) destroying two houses and a shop. In Palgrave Road 106 was hit and at 59, on the corner with Ormond Road, two people were trapped.

The next bomb caused the following message to be sent to the Report Centre:

"Shelter at Hospital School blocked. Four or five people are down there, bomb dropped near."

An underground shelter in the school playground had a near miss. The Warden was later able to get the people out unaided; none was seriously hurt although some were suffering from shock.

A cottage at the Fisherman's Hospital, on the north west corner of the building, was demolished by a direct hit but the occupants were not seriously hurt. Two more bombs fell very close to the church, doing little damage.

Fish Street, Palgrave Road and Ormond Road were closed as a result of this raid and an unexploded high-explosive bomb was later found at the rear of 48 Northgate Street. This was a raid that caused a lot of damage and injury but many people had lucky escapes this February evening.

FEBRUARY 13th

3.10pm One injured.

The north end of the town was machine gunned. Beaconsfield Road Coal Yard and the level crossing were hit and a man living in Churchill Road was injured by a bullet.

16 minutes later eight high-explosive bombs fell on the South Denes, causing no damage.

FEBRUARY 14th

8.01pm One injured.

For several hours on this February evening the sky over East Anglia was filled with the noise of enemy bombers, flares and searchlights lighting up the night sky. During the height of this activity four high-explosive bombs were dropped on Colmans Wharf, totally destroying the quay heading, and another on the marshes near the Breydon Bridge.

The following day a Heinkel 111, flying from a base in France, was shot down 15 miles north east of the town by two Spitfires from 222 Squadron.

FEBRUARY 16th

1.11am to 3am Three killed, six injured.

In the first raid of the day 16 high-explosive bombs fell on Suffolk Road and Gorleston North Railway Station. The booking office was put out of action and both the up and down lines damaged. Two houses in Suffolk Road were demolished and one lady killed. Bomb craters in the adjoining fields showed the path of the bombs to Burgh Road where the last one was only 20 feet from an Anderson shelter. Two women in the cottage were severely shaken but not hurt.

At 2.20am 12 high-explosive bombs fell on the Southtown marshes.

The result of 4 high explosive bombs falling on Colmans Wharf during the evening of February 14th 1941.

At 2.38am more bombs fell across Regent Road. Numbers 4 and 5 Queens Place, Albion Road were hit and rescue workers took over an hour to release the trapped occupants, two of whom were dead and five injured.

A nearby public house had all its windows blown out and part of the roof destroyed but the following day a notice read: *"This blasted pub will open at 12 o'clock."*

An unexploded bomb was found in the garden of 92 Albion Road and the road was closed until it was made safe. One bomb exploded in an open space behind Wickens Pram Shop on Regent Road, wrecked outbuildings and blew out many windows. In houses facing Regent Road, shafts of glass like swords were found the next day driven into the woodwork and the blast caused much structural damage.

At 3am two more German planes approached the town but were driven off by intensive anti-aircraft fire, a bomb dropping in the sea off Gorleston causing no damage.

The next day a Junkers 88, from a base in France, was shot down off Yarmouth by Spitfires of 222 Squadron.

FEBRUARY 18th

3.01am to 5.54am One killed, 12 injured.

This raid could be described as a miniature 'blitz', for German bombers made several separate attacks dropping a total of 28 high-explosive bombs and, although damage was widespread and two large fires were started, the casualty list was remarkably low.

At the first sound of the approaching planes the searchlights pierced the sky and ground defences went into action. In the early morning moonlight the raiders could be clearly seen, many flying very low. One plane, caught in a concentration of searchlights and harassed by anti-aircraft fire, dropped a stick of bombs which set fire to Johnson's Oilskin Factory on the corner of Admiralty Road. The fire rapidly gained hold and was not under control for some two hours, the flames attracting other planes which dropped a number of bombs damaging houses and commercial property in Admiralty and Southgate Roads. Five of the injured in this raid were from one family, a mother and four children. A cooper's works received a direct hit, hot splinters from the bomb setting fire to other nearby property.

As a precaution the Wardens and police quickly evacuated houses and directed people to a shelter at a school. The Royal Naval Training School, HMS *Walrond* on Southgates Road, was destroyed and the road itself closed. Extensive damage was done from the Electricity Works to the Trinity House Store. Other bombs were dropped on the Fishwharf area, causing no damage.

At 5.44am splinters from a high-explosive bomb penetrated the number three gasholder at the Gas Works. The escaping gas immediately caught alight, giving concern that the gasholder would explode. However, a concentration of water from hoses on the supporting uprights prevented buckling, allowing the holder to gradually submerge into the water at the base as the gas escaped. Until this was accomplished the whole area, as a result of the fires, was well illuminated and presented an excellent target for other planes still in the vicinity. It was not until March 14th that the number five gasholder was patched up and the number three holder had to be entirely rebuilt.

Newcastle Road and Beccles Road were hit in this raid and four bombs hit the trawler basin in the Harbour. In Ordnance Road a public shelter was hit, trapping the two occupants. A crater closed Middle Road West and opposite 28 Beccles Road a gas main was fractured. One hundred incendiary bombs fell on the Cobholm marshes.

The German High Command Communique the following day read:

Johnson's Oilskin Factory, Admiralty Road, February 18th 1941

"Bombers successfully attacked important War Objectives in the British Isles. Bomb hits caused fires and destruction in Harbour Installations on the East Coast. A low level attack on Industrial Works SE of Hull resulted in heavy explosions from direct hits. On the Moray Firth in the north of Scotland an oil depot was set on fire... Other solo attacks were directed against Harbour works of Southampton, Great Yarmouth and Sheerness. German bombers attacked an aerodrome on the East Coast of England and scored several hits on a hanger. Violent explosions followed. Some searchlight positions were also bombed."

It had indeed been a busy night for both the Luftwaffe and the British defences.

FEBRUARY 27th
8.15am to 2.13pm Two killed, 22 injured.

The first attack came at breakfast time when a single plane dropped two high-explosive bombs, one onto soft ground in front of a row of cottages, the other scoring a direct hit on the Aquarium public house on the corner of St Nicholas Road and Nelson Road North. The landlord and his family were trapped in the cellar where they had been sleeping. Rescue workers were guided to them by tapping, and all were rescued uninjured.

An eyewitness described how he saw the enemy plane flying from north to south dropping bombs. "It came back from the south and ground defences went

The aftermath of a raid on February 27th 1941. The Aquarium Public House on the corner of Euston and Nelson Roads was demolished, the landlord and his family being rescued unharmed from the cellar some hours later.

At 2.13pm a Junkers 88, based in France, dropped 13 high-explosive bombs in a line east to west from Apsley Road to King Street. Damage was done all along this line and many houses and shops lost their windows and had roofs damaged, particularly in Kent Square, and many people were made homeless.

On the corner of Apsley Road and Rodney Road the garage of Reynolds was destroyed by a direct hit and in York Road another direct hit demolished a house killing a mother and daughter. The Girls' High School and the Manual School were damaged.

An AFS man whose house was wrecked told the local reporter "I was standing at the window and saw a bomb enter the earth like a long silver sausage with fins. I leapt to the other side of the room and lifted an armchair and held it over my wife."

Deneside and St Peters Plain suffered damage and bombs also fell near the Old White Lion public house in King Street and behind Goode's Hotel on the Marine Parade. One of these broke windows in the Sailors' Home. An unexploded bomb was later found opposite 8 York Road.

The ground defences opened fire on this lone raider and it quickly made out to sea, but not before it had caused a lot of damage.

into action, I saw them score a hit on the plane and then they ceased to fire as a Spitfire dived on its tail. The German plane appeared to be in trouble."

Later in the morning a Heinkel 111 flew in so low it seemed as if it would touch the flag pole on the Town Hall. It dropped two high-explosive bombs in the harbour but the anti-aircraft guns caused it to take evasive action and it turned out to sea. There were also two attacks of machine gunning near midday, one on the Royal Naval Hospital, the other over the town generally.

These houses in York Road suffered a direct hit in the afternoon raid of February 27th 1941.

Reynolds Garage on the corner of Apsley and Rodney Roads suffered a direct hit during the afternoon of February 27th 1941. Photo Great Yarmouth Library

MARCH 1st

10.55pm No casualties.

The Wardens reported flares being dropped across the town as a prelude to this raid in which two bombs fell. One landed in the back garden of a house in Exmouth Road while the other fell near the empty Fishwharf Refreshment Rooms public house.

It would appear that the objective of this raid was the Gas Works but both bombs missed their target and damage was limited to the quayside railway lines and some trucks.

MARCH 3rd

11.09pm Three injured

There was considerable air activity over East Anglia during the night and many parachute flares were seen. A single plane was responsible for the raid on Yarmouth, dropping 30 incendiary bombs on Palgrave Brown's Timber Yard and the ABC Wharf.

MARCH 4th

00.18am No casualties.

Two high-explosive and 30 incendiary bombs were dropped on Gorleston, from Bridge Road to Marine Parade. At Gorleston Holiday Camp many wooden chalets were set on fire, but were quickly put out by AFS teams.

MARCH 6th

4.05pm One injured.

Ten bombs were dropped in this raid by a solitary Dornier 17Z, the only casualties being a dozen chickens on allotments near Jellicoe Road. Ground defences drove off the attacker but not before it had machine-gunned houses on Collingwood Road and the railway signal box on Salisbury Road.

Earlier in the day, at 6.43am, one high-explosive bomb had fallen in the river.

The following day another Dornier 17Z was shot down into the sea off Gorleston. The plane had flown in from the sea at a height of about 800 feet when it was met by intense fire from the Bren guns and Bofors guns situated on the sea front. An eyewitness said "I saw the bomber approach and a Bren gun close to me started to fire. I could see the tracer-bullets going into the body of the plane. It apparently caught fire and dived towards the sea." Two members of the crew were rescued by a motor launch.

At 5.22pm 12 high-explosive bombs fell into the sea off the Britannia Pier.

MARCH 8th

10.33am No casualties.

A raider circled the town several times before dropping bombs near the Roman Catholic cemetery on Caister Road and on the Golf Course. No damage was done and other bombs fell in the sea off Britannia Pier.

A Junkers 88 was later shot down about ten miles south east of Yarmouth.

MARCH 15th

00.15am One injured.

30 incendiary and four high-explosive bombs were dropped over various areas of the town. Haylett's Garage

in Northgate Street was hit as were houses in Palgrave Road. The only casualty was in a house on Southtown Road where many houses were damaged near the Rumbold Arms public house.

Incendiaries also fell in Fellow's Shipbuilding Yard. Many people recalled having narrow escapes, as did an ambulance attendant asleep near her ambulance when an incendiary fell beside the bed; it set fire to some stretchers but prompt action saved a serious outbreak.

MARCH 18th

5.27am No casualties.

Early in the morning a German bomber flew over the town with a British fighter in pursuit. The bomber jettisoned its load, eight high-explosive bombs falling on allotments at Runham Vauxhall, the only casualties once again being some chickens. The raider disappeared out to sea, the fighter still machine-gunning it.

The ruins of Marks & Spencer's store in King Street, March 8th 1941.

Many shops in King Street were destroyed in the raid of March 8th 1941, one of the worst raids of the war. Photo Great Yarmouth Library

MARCH 25th

7.50am No casualties.

An empty house near Gorleston Hospital was destroyed when two high-explosive bombs fell in the garden. Windows were damaged at the Hospital and at the nearby Police Station.

MARCH 26th

3.59pm and 7.42pm One injured.

Six high-explosive bombs fell in the sea off Gorleston Pier in the late afternoon followed by another eight off the harbour mouth later in the evening.

MARCH 29th

2.10pm and 5pm No casualties.

Parts of the town were machine-gunned early in the afternoon and at tea time eight high-explosive bombs fell in the sea off the north end of the town.

Illustrations from the ARP Practical Guide.

30

1941 – APRIL, A MONTH OF DESTRUCTION

There is no doubt that the month of April was the worst month of the war for the town of Great Yarmouth. Half the total fatalities for the year were accounted for in this one month, a month when the town lost many of its historic buildings, the great majority of the museum collections and a large area of the unique Rows. Large department stores and small corner shops were burnt out, a considerable number of homes destroyed or damaged and the townscape changed for all time.

On April 1st two high-explosive bombs were dropped into the sea off Gorleston. These caused no damage but three days later the bombers returned.

APRIL 4th

9pm to 11.30pm Three injured.

For two and a half hours there was considerable air activity over the town. Two high-explosive bombs fell in the sea off the harbour mouth and approximately 500 incendiary bombs were dropped over the north end of the Borough in an area from Newtown to Runham Vauxhall by a Junkers 88.

One incendiary which fell through the window of a fruiterer's shop in Northgate Street was quickly extinguished by hand but many of the incendiaries used in this raid were of the explosive type. A large number fell on the Collingwood Road area and on the Racecourse. Prompt action by householders, wardens and the police prevented much damage and this was the night of the stirrup pump.

APRIL 8th

00.10am to 6am 17 killed, 68 injured.

This attack marked the beginning of a series of very heavy raids which caused widespread damage, carried out by Junkers 88s and Heinkel 111s from several Luftwaffe units.

Flares heralded the start of the raid and incendiary bombs were dropped on open ground to the west of the town. These were followed by two parachute mines in the Collingwood Road area which caused considerable damage, undoubtedly dropped by a Heinkel 111. Their bomb load on such raids always included two mines which were primarily intended for shipping lanes but were sometimes, either accidentally or deliberately, dropped over land. Each mine contained about 1000 kg of high explosive and as they exploded above the ground the full force of the explosion was taken by the buildings in their path, causing the maximum damage when dropped over a residential area.

These mines were followed by a huge shower of incendiary bombs falling over an area from the Market Place, across the Row area along South Quay to Gorleston. Within a few minutes the Report Centre was inundated with fire reports from all over the southern half of the Borough. All fire fighting units were soon involved and at 2.08am assistance was requested from Lowestoft and Beccles, followed at 2.57am by a further request to the Regional Office who directed units from the Norwich and Cromer districts to the town.

By now the whole town was lit up and it was said that a newspaper could be read a mile away from the centre of the blaze. In some parts of the town however, visibility was only 20 feet owing to the density of the smoke. To add to the difficulties of the fire fighters,

A typical Yarmouth Row. Many of these unique 'streets' were destroyed during the war, particularly in the Middlegate area of the town in April 1941.

hostile planes continued to drop incendiaries over the area, causing further fires. In all 65 major and 200 smaller fires raged, the results of 4000 incendiary bombs.

At the height of the fires burning across the Row area, a stick of high-explosive bombs fell on Southtown Road, causing craters and cutting off Yarmouth from Gorleston. The Warden Post in Baker Street reported "Southtown Road quite impossible to do anything tonight, so must be considered blocked to traffic." A water main was broken, resulting in a considerable reduction in the pressure available in the town.

The assistance from other districts duly arrived and good progress was being made in controlling the fires when, at 5.02am, two parachute mines fell, one at the junction of Blackfriars Road and Queens Road, the other at the south end of Middlegate Street.

The first destroyed the Seagull Garage which was used as a Special Constabulary Station, killing five Special Constables, and caused a lot of damage in the surrounding area. The second mine, falling on the Row area, caused so much damage the Report Centre had to request three Rescue Parties from Norwich as well as Military assistance to clear the debris. The flames from the burning buildings illuminated the devastation caused by the mine and buildings collapsed like a pack of cards, burning gas mains sending up columns of fire as smoke and dust shrouded the ruined buildings.

As dawn broke the streets were filled with rubble and miles of hose pipe, weary firemen damping down smouldering buildings while groups of soldiers dug for survivors and tried to clear some streets. Ambulances and Mobile Canteens made their way through the debris and the air was filled with the acrid smell of burning. Over 400 people were made homeless and at least 300 houses were unfit for habitation, resulting in the Rest Centres and Feeding Centres being stretched to their limits.

Many well known shops and other properties were destroyed or damaged. Those gutted by fire included Marks & Spencers, Rose's Fashion Shop, Kerridges, Jarrolds, Boots, Maypole Dairy, Hills Restaurant, Greens, Marsh's Pawnbrokers, Sullivans and Halfords all in King Street. Partly damaged property included the corner of Palmers Mens Shop, Moy's Coal Office, Fletchers Opticians, the Freeman Hardy & Willis shoe shop at the top of the Arcade, Arcade Chemists and Hellingsworths.

The Tolhouse Museum, Library, Science School and Mission to Seamen were severely damaged and Johnsons Factory in Middlegate Street gutted. Other property destroyed included Masons Laundry and the Seagull Garage in Queens Road.

This picture was taken on the night of April 7th/8th 1941 when large areas were set alight by 4000 incendiary bombs. Photo Imperial War Museum

At 9.30pm the enemy returned, dropping four high-explosive bombs at the south end of the town and later many incendiary bombs on premises both side of the river. The Salt Union store was gutted but other fires were soon extinguished, preventing a repetition of the previous nights destruction.

APRIL 9th

2.32am Six killed, five injured.

The first high-explosive bombs of this raid fell on the south beach and in the river causing no damage but at 3.07am another four high-explosive bombs were dropped on Nile Road and Upper Cliff Road, Gorleston. At 51 Nile Road a family were killed when their Anderson shelter, in which they were sleeping, was destroyed. A total of ten houses were destroyed and many others damaged in this raid.

APRIL 10th

11.10pm to 1.30am Two killed, three injured.

The first attack of this raid resulted in two high-explosive bombs falling on the Springfield Road and Bells Road area of Gorleston causing the above casualties, the two people killed being in their shelter at 138 Upper Bells Road.

At 1.29am the second attack was made on the sea front and 16 high-explosive bombs fell in a line from Nelson Road Central to the North Drive. Little damage was caused as all the bombs failed to explode. One fell on the Royal Aquarium Theatre, one in the centre of Norfolk Square and another outside the Victoria Dairy on Nelson Road. Four landed on the North Drive and one outside the Queens Hotel. At 69 Crown Road one bomb fell right through the house and outside Hills Marine View Hotel one lodged in the bushes. The only damage was to a water main on North Drive.

APRIL 11th

00.17am 13 killed, 12 injured.

A heavily populated part of the town, George Street and North Quay, was hit by four high-explosive bombs. One fell on a public shelter, killing seven occupants. Rescue work began immediately here and among the ruins of surrounding houses and continued until midday, the following message being sent to the Report Centre by the police:

"Send demolition squad, George Street. Terrible mess."

At the end of Row 33 a gas main was broken and caught fire and in George Street a water main burst. Over 50 houses were destroyed and rescue squads helped many people out of the rubble. A further 100 houses were so badly damaged they had to be demolished and the towns emergency services worked throughout the next day to provide shelter for the homeless and patch up at least another 200 houses.

The apparent objective of this raid was either the Haven Bridge or the wood yards for the bombs fell in a direct line towards them, the raider having released his load seconds too soon.

APRIL 16th

00.08am to 5.18am Two killed, 19 injured.

This raid was carried out by Dornier 17Z aircraft from a base in France and consisted of five separate attacks.

In the first of these two high-explosive bombs fell on the seafront causing damage to property. The second attack came soon after with incendiary bombs falling in the centre of the town causing small fires which were quickly extinguished by the Wardens and Fire Parties. Incendiaries fell on the roofs of the Regal Cinema, Woolworths, the Peace and Plenty public house in South Market Road and the Electric House in Regent Road.

Two parachute mines were dropped, one landing on the marshes west of the river and the other at the junction of Alderson and Palgrave Roads, causing considerable damage to houses here and in Northgate Street, Lawn Avenue and Salisbury Road.

The fourth attack was on Row 132 and South Quay, where four high-explosive bombs fell. Mr Blackrun's house at number 15 Row 132 vibrated with the blast, then collapsed. After the morning sun had risen a lone raider returned to the town and dropped two high-explosive bombs on 31 and 39 Bells Marsh Road, Gorleston. Dock Tavern Lane was blocked by a crater and a further two bombs fell in the vicinity of Messrs Crabtrees' Yard, Southtown.

APRIL 17th

3.05am No casualties.

A stick of eight high-explosive bombs were dropped on Beccles Road, near Church Lane, Gorleston. The Yarmouth Mercury report the following day read:

"Early yesterday morning a solitary raider dropped a string of bombs on the outskirts of an East Coast town. There were no casualties, and the only damage was to a bungalow, which was demolished by a direct hit. The occupants were sleeping elsewhere."

Mission Road, Cobholm, after the raid of April 18th 1941.

APRIL 18th

5.19am 12 killed, 13 injured.

Five enemy planes, flying in at a low altitude, dropped eight high-explosive bombs, two of which fell on the Coronation Road and Elsie Road area of Cobholm. Several houses in Elsie Road, 21,22,25,26 and 27, were either destroyed or damaged. In one the only member of a family of six to be rescued alive was a 12 year old boy, Wilfred Wright. Three people in a garden shelter had a lucky escape; an almost direct hit left them sitting on the edge of a crater.

APRIL 23rd

9.08pm Two injured.

A stick of 20 high-explosive bombs was dropped on Gorleston High Street, Duke Road, School Lane, High Street and Blackwall Reach. An empty shop was hit and other business premises were damaged but the Palace Cinema escaped.

The next day four bombs fell on the Southtown marshes and three days later another four fell in the sea north of the harbour mouth.

The Duke found time to inspect a guard of honour oputside the Town Hall. April 25th 1941.

APRIL 28th

8.33am No casualties.

A single Junkers 88 dropped five bombs, four of which fell in the sea whilst the fifth fell in the stable yard of a private house in Southtown Road. Although the stable and other outbuildings were destroyed there were no casualties.

HRH The Duke of Gloucester inspecting bomb damaged areas in Middlegate during his visit on April 25th 1941.

APRIL 29th

9.54pm No casualties.

Three high-explosive bombs were dropped in the area of Burgh Road, Gorleston.

The Luftwaffe had various hand-books with potential land-marks and targets. The pictures were often taken from tourist guides or company brochures.

GB 9, BB 19, Nr. 21: Eisenbahnbrücke in Great Yarmouth (Norfolk).
"Breydon Viaduct", eiserne Drehbrücke der Strecke Yarmouth---Lowestoft (London North Eastern Railw.) über Breydonwater. Trapez-Fachwerkträger; drei feste Überbauten von je 51,8 m, ein Überbau von 33,8 m; der Überbau von zwei Öffnungen ist auf einem gemeinsamen Pfeiler drehbar gelagert. Durchfahrt für Schiffe 18,2 m Breite. Offene Fahrrinne.

Following the heavy raids of April, the year continued with little relief from death and destruction.

The first raider in May dropped eight high-explosive bombs on the marshes west of Caister Road on the night of the 3rd.

MAY 5th

Alert 00.15am to 4.30am No casualties.

Six high-explosive bombs and a number of incendiaries were dropped across the cemetery bordering Kitchener Road and Nelson Road at 4.42am by a raider being chased by a British fighter on this Sunday night. The nearby church of St Nicholas escaped damage although many graves in the cemetery were disturbed.

Earlier in the morning one high-explosive bomb had dropped on Lowestoft Road at Gorleston, damaging shops and houses, although there were no injuries to the inhabitants.

MAY 8th

Alert midnight to 5am No casualties.

After circling over the town for some time a Junkers 88 dropped 22 high-explosive bombs on the area of Stafford Road and Southtown Common at 00.01am. An Anderson shelter took the full force of one bomb but luckily the usual inhabitants had decided to spend that particular night elsewhere. Six houses were damaged or destroyed.

On the same night a Junkers 88 was shot down by 257 Squadron off Lowestoft.

MAY 9th

Alert 00.30am to 1.50am Six killed, ten injured.

Three attacks were made on the town within 90 minutes. The first raider was caught in a concentration of searchlights and as it dived steeply released a stick of ten high-explosive bombs, one of which damaged part of the Isolation Hospital in Escourt Road and another damaging the Rescue Depot at Churchill Road.

In the second attack eight high-explosive bombs dropped on Cobholm, hitting Lady Haven Road and Mill Road. Among the property damaged was the Lady Haven public house, Cobholm Post Office, an Ice Cream Depot and a furniture store. Fires broke out and several houses were damaged but prompt action by the AFS prevented any serious fire. A total of 12 houses and four shops were either damaged or destroyed and among those killed was one family of three, only recently

rehoused after an earlier attack. The Warden post at Watling's Maltings, Steam Mill Lane was hit as were Porter's Saw Mills and houses in Gatacre Road and Granville Road.

The third attack was on a merchant ship that had for some time been beached at the south end of the town. This ship was attacked many times by the Luftwaffe during the year.

MAY 12th

Alert 00.15am to 4.40am Two injured.

During the three hours of this raid six separate attacks were made. Several planes were involved and although 38 high-explosive bombs were dropped and considerable damage done, only two people were injured.

(Postage in United Kingdom 1½d.)   Price 2d.

Duke of Kent Visits Yarmouth

INSPECTION OF RAID DAMAGED AREAS

YARMOUTH on Friday morning last received a visit from the Duke of Kent, who, after inspecting a parade of civil defence workers, toured the areas bombed in the early spring.

The Duke, who was accompanied by the Regional Commissioner, Sir Will Spens, was met at the boundary of the borough by the Chief Constable (Mr. C. G. Box), who led the way to the centre of the town, where the Mayor welcomed him outside the Town Hall. The Mayor (Mr. E. R. Herman) then presented to the Duke the Town Clerk (Mr. Farra Conway), the chairman of the A.R.P. Committee (Mr. A. W. Hollis), the chairman of the Watch Committee (Mr. P. R. Hill). Mr. E. C. H. Freeman (Supervisor of the Report Centre), the Medical Officer of Health (Mr. D. Wainwright), the Deputy Borough Engineer (Mr H. F. Dyson), who is in charge of rescue and demolition squads, and a local organiser of the W.V.S. (Mrs. F. G. Pearson).

CIVIL DEFENCE WORKERS INSPECTED

The Duke, who was in the uniform of a group captain of the R.A.F., inspected civil defence workers outside the Town Hall. He spent nearly half an hour over this, and also spoke to nurses, V.A.Ds, rescue parties, firemen, first aid workers and wardens.

He asked one woman warden how long she had been in the A.R.P., and she replied that she was one of the first to take the examination.

TALKS WITH WOMEN

When the Duke drove around the bombed areas, although the visit had not been announced, crowds gathered, and the Duke spent a considerable time chatting to women who had lost their homes.

In one district he spoke to the proprietor of a garage which was shattered by a heavy bomb. Here five special constables who were in part of the building were killed.

The proprietor, who is also a special constable, told the Duke that he was on duty in another part of the town at the time, and that his wife was in a shelter at the rear of the garage. The Duke asked what he proposed to do now, and the proprietor replied that he hoped to secure other premises.

AGED FISHERMAN'S STORY

Near by the Duke chatted with an 81-year-old fisherman, who was looking at the ruins of his home in which he had lived 59 years.

The old man explained that he was in bed when the bomb blew out the front of the house, but he escaped with an injured arm.

"I think it is wonderful the way you are standing up to it," commented the Duke on leaving him.

The Duke asked if the bricks from bombed houses were salvaged, and whether the broken woodwork was given to the poor people for firewood.

QUESTION ABOUT CHILDREN

Many of the women who had lost their homes told the Duke that they had husbands and sons in the Army, and several times he asked. "Are you going to send your children away?"

The Duke visited several small shops that had been badly damaged, but where it was "business as usual."

In one little general shop, the proprietor, an Italian, who is now a British subject, took the Duke upstairs and showed him the damage to the roof, and when he left kissed his hand.

He concluded his tour by driving through a shopping centre, where damage had been done.

On May 2nd 1941 the Yarmouth Mercury reported the visit of the Duke of Kent, one of the several visits made by members of the Royal Family to the town during the war years.

Anderson shelters, similar to this one in Wellington Place, saved many lives during the air raids. Photo Great Yarmouth Library

The areas hit were Beaconsfield Road, Caister Road, Northgate Street, the Yacht Station and, in Gorleston, Addison Road, Highfield Road and Cemetery Lane.

The Transport Depot on Caister Road was damaged; apart from the building every bus in the depot was also damaged, some severely. This resulted in the Transport Committee recalling five buses they had loaned to Coventry earlier in the war.

Later in the day a Junkers 88 was destroyed 15 miles north east of the town.

The only bomb dropped in an early morning raid on June 5th 1941. It failed to explode and is seen here in Admiralty Road.

MAY 13th

00.48am Three killed, three injured.

Four high-explosive bombs fell in the area of Colomb Road and High Street Gorleston. One exploded in the yard of Hammonds Ironmongers shop in the High Street while another scored a direct hit on 15 Colomb Road, killing the occupants and burying the next door family under tons of rubble, killing one and injuring the others.

MAY 14th

2.12pm and 7.17pm One injured.

In the early afternoon seven high-explosive bombs fell in the sea and one vessel was sunk but all the crew were saved, one being injured.

Later that day a high-explosive bomb fell on Blackwall Reach, Gorleston.

MAY 16th

2.57am and 4.46am No casualties.

An area from Cemetery Lane to Baliol Road, Gorleston, received ten high-explosive bombs during this raid and later a ship in the harbour, the SS *Ethel Ratcliffe*, was hit in the aft hold.

MAY 24th

8.53pm Three injured.

A single raider dropped four high-explosive bombs on Alexandra Road and St Georges Park. One fell near the Nurses' Home, blowing out every window in the building, while others fell on the east side of the road, causing damage to the War Memorial in the park, damage that can be seen today.

Later in the evening another raider was driven off by the Ground Defences, dropping its bombs in the sea, black smoke pouring from one of its engines.

JUNE 5th

3.40am No casualties.

One high-explosive bomb fell, but failed to explode, in Admiralty Road near Johnson's Oilskin Factory, damaging a water main.

JUNE 12th

Alert 2am to 5am Four killed, one injured.

After circling the town for some time this raider dropped three high-explosive bombs at 2.38am. One scored a direct hit on the Tramway Hotel, Gorleston, and it was here that four people were killed, the landlord and his family.

The leaded windows of Gorleston Library were sucked out by the blast and at the nearby parish church stained glass windows were also damaged. An AFS station near the Tramway Hotel was damaged, the men asleep inside having a lucky escape.

Other bombs fell on Duke Road and Fredrick Road; the latter, a 4000 lb bomb, failed to explode.

At the north end of the town an AFS man was injured during a machine gun attack at 3.20am.

JUNE 15th

1.38pm One injured.

Several bombs were dropped in the High Street to Western Road area of Gorleston, the railway receiving a direct hit. Another bomb landed behind a stonemasons premises and blew in the side of the Lowestoft Road Baptist Church. Unexploded bombs were later found in Roslyn Road, Middleton Road and Western Road.

An Air Ministry communique in the evening stated:
"This afternoon a single enemy aircraft dropped bombs on the East Coast of East Anglia. It did some damage but no one was seriously injured. Apart from this incident there has been nothing to report".

A 4000lb high explosive bomb that failed to explode in Fredrick Road, Gorleston, on June 12th 1941.

These pictures show some of the activity when a Coastal Battery is in action. The 325th Coast Battery, 514th Coast Regiment AA 2nd Corps, at Great Yarmouth in 1941.33

Gun drill. In the foreground a charge is seen being taken from its container. (Next Page)

Bringing the shells by hand to the gun floor.   (right)

Placing the charges on a trolley.   (above)

Action stations — camouflage nets are removed from one of the guns.   (below)

Photos Imperial War Museum

JUNE 17th

Midnight to 1.40am No casualties.

12 high-explosive bombs were dropped in the Caister Road area, from Freemantle Road to the Racecourse at 00.58am and later another four were dropped near the Breydon Railway Bridge.

JUNE 23rd

2.05am No casualties.

Three planes took part in this raid, dropping approximately 200 incendiary bombs in the Newtown area. These caused many small fires that were quickly extinguished by the wardens and householders. Another fire was started at the Smith's Potato Crisp factory on Caister Road. Many of the incendiaries fell on the nearby marshland causing no damage.

JUNE 24th

2.27am and 2.40am One injured.

After circling for some hours the enemy planes dropped flares followed by incendiary and high-explosive bombs.

The first 20 high-explosive bombs fell across the harbour mouth and shortly afterwards about 200 incendiaries and 22 high-explosives fell on south west Gorleston, the intense anti-aircraft fire preventing the raiders from aiming at their intended targets. Many of the bombs fell on open land. Another eight bombs fell across the river from Gorleston to Southtown Gas Works, damaging the retort house and the ABC Wharf.

On the night of July 2nd eight high-explosive bombs fell in the sea off Gorleston.

JULY 5th

Alert 00.45am to 4am No casualties.

During this raid one bomb was dropped on allotments west of Southtown Road followed at 3.40am by 11 high-explosive bombs in the fields off Middleton Road, Gorleston. Ten minutes later four bombs fell on Boundary Road.

JULY 7th

1.04am to 2.59am 12 killed, 6 injured.

There had been no alert before four separate attacks were

Issued by the Ministry of Information *in co-operation with the War Office and the Ministry of Home Security*

Beating the INVADER

A MESSAGE FROM THE PRIME MINISTER

IF invasion comes, everyone—young or old, men and women—will be eager to play their part worthily. By far the greater part of the country will not be immediately involved. Even along our coasts, the greater part will remain unaffected. But where the enemy lands, or tries to land, there will be most violent fighting. Not only will there be the battles when the enemy tries to come ashore, but afterwards there will fall upon his lodgments very heavy British counter-attacks, and all the time the lodgments will be under the heaviest attack by British bombers. The fewer civilians or non-combatants in these areas, the better—apart from essential workers who must remain. So if you are advised by the authorities to leave the place where you live, it is your duty to go elsewhere when you are told to leave. When the attack begins, it will be too late to go ; and, unless you receive definite instructions to move, your duty then will be to stay where you are. You will have to get into the safest place you can find, and stay there until the battle is over. For all of you then the order and the duty will be : " STAND FIRM ".

This also applies to people inland if any considerable number of parachutists or air-borne troops are landed in their neighbourhood. Above all, they must not cumber the roads. Like their fellow-countrymen on the coasts, they must " STAND FIRM ". The Home Guard, supported by strong mobile columns wherever the enemy's numbers require it, will immediately come to grips with the invaders, and there is little doubt will soon destroy them.

Throughout the rest of the country where there is no fighting going on and no close cannon fire or rifle fire can be heard, everyone will govern his conduct by the second great order and duty, namely, " CARRY ON ". It may easily be some weeks before the invader has been totally destroyed, that is to say, killed or captured to the last man who has landed on our shores. Meanwhile, all work must be continued to the utmost, and no time lost.

The following notes have been prepared to tell everyone in rather more detail what to do, and they should be carefully studied. Each man and woman should think out a clear plan of personal action in accordance with the general scheme.

Winston S. Churchill

STAND FIRM

1. What do I do if fighting breaks out in my neighbourhood?

Keep indoors or in your shelter until the battle is over. If you can have a trench ready in your garden or field, so much the better. You may want to use it for protection if your house is damaged. But if you are at work, or if you have special orders, carry on as long as possible and only take cover when danger approaches. If you are on your way to work, finish your journey if you can.

If you see an enemy tank, or a few enemy soldiers, do not assume that the enemy are in control of the area. What you have seen may be a party sent on in advance, or stragglers from the main body who can easily be rounded up.

made on the town in the early hours of this Monday morning. Four high-explosive bombs were dropped, three in a cluster, in the area of Frederick and Kitchener Roads. Five Anderson shelters suffered a direct hit, killing seven occupants; a shop was destroyed and the Coach and Horses public house on the corner of Kitchener Road was badly damaged. Stone's Nurseries on Northgate Street were destroyed. The Rescue Squads were soon on the scene and worked by moonlight to release people from the many damaged houses. At daybreak the area presented a desolate scene, women's stockings and other clothing festooned on telegraph wires and a couch, hurled from a wrecked house, was lodged on the roof of a garage.

In the second attack four high-explosive bombs fell at Southgates Road, demolishing a ship's chandler's store and a house. Several other houses were damaged but there were no reported casualties.

One heavy high-explosive bomb was then dropped on Row 127 and the iron foundry of Messrs Brett was demolished, together with eight houses.

In the last attack of the morning four high-explosive bombs were dropped to the west of Southtown Road and the Rumbold Arms public house was damaged.

resultant fires attracted other bombers to the target but the subsequent bombs put out the fires started by the first ones.

At the height of the raids showers of pamphlets, referring to the 'lost battle of the Atlantic' "fell like snowflakes", according to a special constable who was on duty at the time.

On Caister Road a large water main was fractured and on the South Quay 40 yards of quay heading fell into the river.

The Report Centre called for assistance from Norwich in an attempt to clear the streets and as dawn broke the WVS and Salvation Army teams toured the streets with hot drinks for the homeless and the rescue parties.

Unexploded bombs were found at Crabtrees' Shipyard, Colman's Wharf and in Beevor Road. It was estimated that 120 houses had been demolished and over 1,000 damaged during this raid. The small number of casualties was remarkable, even considering the reduced population owing to evacuation, and the morale of the townsfolk remained remarkably high.

JULY 9th

Alert 00.20am to 4.25am Three killed, 29 injured.

This raid was one of the heaviest of the whole war period. During some 21 separate attacks 80 high-explosive bombs, ranging from 50 kilos to 1,800 kilos, and approximately 1,000 incendiary bombs were dropped, as well as a quantity of propaganda leaflets. The first bombs fell at 1.05am and all parts of the Borough were involved during the next two hours, including Caister Road, Kitchener Road, Crown Road, St Peters Plain, Southtown Road, Anson Road, Rows 92 to 101, South Quay, Beccles Road, Burgh Road, Blackwall Reach, Suffling Road and Southtown Station.

Jewson's Timber Yard and the nearby Sefton Arms public house in Sefton Lane were severely damaged, fire breaking out in the timber yard. In Middlegate Street the Unitarian Chapel and a number of houses were destroyed, causing many injuries. At Southtown Station a direct hit damaged both main lines, holding up all traffic, and several carriages were overturned. One of the gas holders at the Southtown Gas Works was hit.

The Nurses' Home on Alexandra Road once again had all the windows blown in and numbers 9, 10 and 11 Crown Road were destroyed. The Baptist Chapel was damaged and a shelter in the park, housing 30 people, had a near miss. Another bomb fell near the Report Centre at the Art School but emergency lighting was brought into use and the Centre continued to operate.

A line of incendiary bombs were dropped on the huts and nets of the fishermen on the South Denes. The

JULY 11th

Alert 00.50am to 5am One killed, seven injured.

This was another raid with four separate attacks, the first on Lowestoft Road at 1.04am where two high-explosive bombs fell and then on Church Road and Duke Road, the East Anglian school being damaged.

A bomb on Bells Marsh Road killed one person and Fellow's Shipyard was hit. The last attack was on Granville Road, Cobholm, where three high-explosive bombs fell. In all 15 houses were destroyed, 25 badly damaged and 390 slightly damaged during this raid.

JULY 14th

3.21am Six killed, 12 injured.

No alert was given before a single bomber dropped four high-explosive bombs, estimated to weigh 250 kg, on Mill Road and St Lukes Terrace, Cobholm. 20 houses were demolished or damaged together with St Lukes Church and Institute, which had been in use as a Rest Centre. Luckily the last of the people who had been sheltering there following an earlier raid had been moved out only a few hours earlier.

The Home Guard, police and neighbours joined the rescue squads and toiled for many hours before all the trapped people were released.

JULY 21st

00.10am and 00.28am No casualties.

Four high-explosive bombs fell in the sea, soon to be followed by another four falling on North Drive. Although some damage was caused, there were no casualties.

JULY 23rd

Alert 11.38pm to 2.38am 11 injured.

12 high-explosive bombs fell in the Newtown area at 1.55am, across Keys and Balmoral Avenues, Caister Road and Tennyson Road. All fell in gardens or on the roads and no houses were directly hit although 120 were damaged together with two shops and a school.

Two days later more high-explosive bombs fell in the sea.

The damaged Gorleston and Southtown Gas Works after the raid of July 9th 1941. During this heavy raid on the town over 1000 incendiary bombs were dropped.

A series of public information leaflets was issued to every household.

JULY 28th

11.33pm Five injured.

Five soldiers, members of the crew of an anti-aircraft gun at the south end of the Marine Parade, were injured when eight high-explosive bombs fell across the Nelson Gardens bowling greens and boating lake. There was no damage to property.

On August 7th another eight high-explosive bombs fell into the sea.

AUGUST 7th

Alert 10.30pm to 4.45am No casualties.

A lone raider dropped four high-explosive bombs in the Caister Road and North Denes area at 002.44am. Several private houses and 'Mason Doone' hairdressers in Salisbury Road were demolished although there were no casualties. The family living next door to the hairdressers managed to take cover under the stairs before the bomb exploded. The blast caused most of the ceilings to fall down and filled the house with bricks and rubble.

At 00.56am two high-explosive bombs fell in the river near the Haven Bridge, doing no damage and later in the night another four fell in the sea.

Further bombs fell in the sea on the nights of August 14th, 15th, 16th and 17th.

AUGUST 19th

Alert 4.30am to 5.10am Six injured.

At 3.56am ten high-explosive bombs were dropped in the Baker Street and Blackwall Reach area of Gorleston, the injured being in an Anderson shelter hit by splinters. A direct hit was suffered by the Waterside Tavern, on the corner of Baker Street, a public house owned by Mr Johnson, a former lifeboat coxswain.

A ship was sunk later in the month when six high-explosive bombs were dropped in the sea.

SEPTEMBER 7th

Alert 9.45pm to 1.38am No casualties.

Four high-explosive bombs were dropped near the Breydon Railway Bridge in this raid at 11.31pm, causing some damage to the bridge and railway lines. This necessitated a 10mph speed restriction until the line was repaired.

SEPTEMBER 21st

2.44am One injured.

Eight high-explosive bombs were dropped on St Peters Road, Lancaster Road and York Road. Many failed to explode and only minimal damage was caused. The one casualty was Mr Bean, injured by a tile dislodged when a bomb penetrated his roof of his house. The bomb ended up embedded into the ground on his front door step where it fractured a gas main but did not explode.

50 incendiaries were dropped on South Beach Parade, causing no damage.

More bombs fell in the sea during the evening of September 25th, off Gorleston, when a raider was driven away by searchlights and guns and again on October 3rd off the South Denes.

Illustrations from Air Raids Precautions Handbooks 1 and 2.

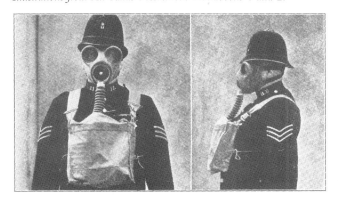

OCTOBER 11th

7.40pm No casualties.

A single raider dropped four high-explosive bombs, one falling on Juby's Builders Yard, Southtown Road, damaging Nos 247, 248 and 249 Southtown Road. Two of the houses were empty and the builder's family who lived in the other were sleeping elsewhere that night. Another property, Fairhead House, was destroyed by a direct hit.

On South Quay, near the Mission for Seamen Institute, a group of communal shelters were hit but luckily they were empty.

One bomb, which failed to explode, passed through the stern of the SS *Nessus*, moored at the quay.

Four high-explosive bombs fell in the sea off the South Denes at 1.15am on October 13th.

OCTOBER 16th

Alert 3.00am to 5.20am No casualties.

At 3.20am one mine and one high-explosive bomb were dropped harmlessly in a lane and a field at Wood Farm Lane, Gorleston. At 4.18am a plane, flying only a few hundred feet above the town, dropped four high-explosive bombs on Southgates Road, damaging the offices of Bloomfields.

OCTOBER 18th

7.29pm Two injured.

A Dornier was responsible for this raid in which a number of houses were severely damaged in the area of Raleigh Avenue, Beatty Road, Blake Road, Tennyson Road and Sandringham Avenue.

Barnard Bridge was hit and made unsafe but this was quickly repaired and the army detachment resumed the manning of the anti-aircraft gun placed upon the bridge.

The two people injured in this raid were a man blown off his bicycle by the blast and a Mrs Cooper, sheltering in her Morrison shelter, when her house was hit.

OCTOBER 30th

6.52pm No casualties.

12 planes of 257 Squadron scrambled from Coltishall against a force of 20 Junkers 88s which was detected approaching the East Coast. A single Junkers 88 detached itself from the main force and dive-bombed the town, dropping four high-explosive bombs on Micawber Avenue and Admiralty Road. In Micawber Avenue numbers 9, 11 and 13 were destroyed and Mason's Laundry on Queens Road was badly damaged. The corner of St James School was destroyed and houses in Newcastle Road damaged.

The raider was met by ground fire and although it circled the town again flew out to sea without doing further damage.

The following day, between 6.22pm and 7.01pm, three sticks of high-explosive bombs were dropped in the sea off the South Denes. This happened again the following day at 10.54pm and was repeated on November 2nd between 6.57pm and 8.22pm.

NOVEMBER 7th

10.14pm No casualties.

Four high-explosive bombs fell in the Cobholm area, one scoring a direct hit on the M & GN Railway line. The Breydon Junction signal box was damaged.

NOVEMBER 10th

Alert 12.20pm to 5.30pm No casualties.

12 high-explosive bombs fell along the beach at the South Denes, doing no damage. Unexploded bombs were later found near 34 North Drive and close to the Grammar School in Salisbury Road. A merchant ship was machine-gunned at sea.

NOVEMBER 18th

6.45pm No casualties.

One high-explosive bomb fell on the Roman Catholic Cemetery, Caister Road. The previous day more bombs had fallen in the sea off the harbour mouth.

Most major towns and cities held special fund-raising weeks. Here Norwich is the target, to adopt HMS Norfolk.

NORWICH WARSHIP WEEK

JANUARY 31ST TO FEBRUARY 7TH 1942

OUR TARGET £1,000,000

NORWICH SAVINGS COMMITTEE,
SUCKLING HOUSE,
ST. ANDREW'S HILL,
NORWICH.
19th January, 1942

Dear Sir or Madam,

You will probably be aware that it has been decided to hold a Warship Week in Norwich from 31st January to 7th February.

The aim is to raise £1,000,000 through the various investments mentioned overleaf and the total will be devoted by His Majesty's Government towards the cost of a Warship.

A successful outcome to our efforts is only possible with your whole-hearted and enthusiastic support, and you are very strongly urged to invest to your utmost during the period and to persuade your friends and employees to render similar service.

Providing the financial target is reached the Admiralty will permit the "adoption" of H.M.S. "Norfolk" by the community and we feel that this will afford an additional incentive to enable our ambitious aim to be accomplished, whilst should you require any advice or assistance it will be readily forthcoming at the Selling Centres, included amongst which are the Branches of:

Barclays Bank, Ltd.   National Provincial Bank, Ltd.
Lloyds Bank, Ltd.   Westminster Bank, Ltd.
Midland Bank, Ltd.   Post Office Savings Bank.
       East Anglian Trustee Savings Bank.

On behalf of the Committee, who appeal to you with every confidence for your maximum contribution to this portion of the National Effort,

Yours faithfully,

J. H. Barnes
Lord Mayor of Norwich.

Herbert W. Gowen
Chairman of Norwich Savings Committee.

GIVE THE NELSON TOUCH TO NORWICH WARSHIP WEEK

1942 – THE RAIDS EASE

The town experienced fewer raids in 1942, 26 compared with 167 the previous year. There were 324 Alerts and the casualties for the year were 27 killed and 95 injured.

A British Restaurant, designed to provide good, plain, cheap food at lunchtime, was opened in the Market Place, in the old Angel Hotel and in May agreement was reached with the Education Committee to start a school meals service, the meals provided by the restaurant.

This was also the year of the scrap metal campaigns and many ornamental iron railings were removed from front gardens all over the Borough, never to be replaced.

During the year the parish church was destroyed as was the Corporation refuse destructor. Despite the continued bombing of the town the Council began to consider post-war redevelopment plans and how to restore the town as a holiday resort. One of the proposals discussed was for a stadium to be built, near the Borough boundary, on Caister Road.

The town bus service, already reduced to the three basic war-time routes, Market Place to Caister, Newtown to Fishwharf and Theatre Plain to Gorleston, was further hit by fuel shortages. One in every three bus stops was eliminated and queuing became the order of the day.

JANUARY 21st

6.05pm No casualties.

There was no warning before this first raid of the year and two high-explosive bombs were dropped on Common Road and Alpha Road, Southtown. Damage was done to the Slipper Factory and a services lorry was destroyed. Two houses in Alpha Road were badly damaged.

On February 5th four high-explosive bombs fell in the sea at 9.12am.

The old Angel Hotel in the Market Place which was used as the British Restaurant from 1942.

FEBRUARY 18th

12.50pm Eight killed, five injured.

A Dornier 217, flying from a base in Holland, suddenly appeared out of the clouds at lunch time and dropped four high-explosive bombs on Northgate Street and Rampart Road. Northgate Street was cratered and closed to traffic. Most of those killed and injured were in the Refuge Insurance office, a three story building in Northgate Street which was demolished by a direct hit.

One person was killed in the house next door and two more in a nearby cottage that was reduced to a pile of rubble by the blast. As the raid came in the middle of the day a great number of people were on the streets and saw the bombs leave the plane. Police, firemen and soldiers joined in the rescue work and Bren Gun carriers were used to carry away the debris. The owner of a garage spoke of how he was lying on his back under a car when he heard the rattle of machine gun fire. He scrambled up but before he could take cover he was thrown against a wall, the roof of the garage being completely blown off.

In this raid 20 houses were seriously damaged and another 150 suffered superficial damage.

MARCH 8th

10.51pm No casualties.

Two parachute mines were dropped on the Cobholm marshes, near the Breydon Railway Bridge. One exploded, the blast breaking windows in Lichfield Road and as far away as Regent Street, where Arnolds Store was affected.

The other mine failed to explode and was found half out of the ground with its parachute still attached only 40 yards from the railway line. The Beach Station to Lowestoft line had to be closed until the Naval Bomb Disposal Squad had defused the mine.

MARCH 28th

00.07am No casualties.

A single plane dropped four high-explosive bombs on the beach and North Drive, the only damage being to a few windows in private houses and an ornamental shelter.

MAY 30th

Alert 1.20am to 3.47am

Three killed, three injured.

This raid was carried out by six Dornier 217 aircraft based in Holland, in bright moonlight.

The results of an early morning raid on Albany Road, May 30th 1942.

49

The high explosive bomb that fell on the Pleasure Beach, May 30th 1942. This bomb now stands outside the Maritime Museum on Marine Parade, used as a collecting box. Photo P Trett

At 1.16am a single high-explosive bomb fell on the South Denes, close to the Admiralty petrol storage tanks.

At 2.34am a shelter at Jewson's Timber Yard was hit and two men killed. Rescue work took several hours before the bodies could be recovered. 1 and 12 Albany Road were hit by another bomb, a woman being killed in number 12. Two houses were demolished and 39 damaged in the area and several large trees were uprooted. The raiders could be clearly seen in the moonlight with shells from the ground defences bursting around them.

At 3.01am two high-explosive bombs were dropped on Nelson Gardens, Marine Parade and destroyed a military post. Another bomb was later found unexploded in the Pleasure Beach. (Today this bomb stands outside the Maritime Museum at Great Yarmouth, where it is used as a collecting box.)

During the night aircraft from 68 Squadron claimed a Dornier 217 and damaged a Junkers 88. Squadron Leader Howden shot down a Dornier 217 and Flight Lieutenant Windward shot down a Junkers 88, both pilots flying Beaufighters from Coltishall.

The same moon that illuminated Yarmouth for the Dornier 217s also shed its light on the German city of Cologne for the first 1000 bomber raid. The following day the Yarmouth Report Centre received a message:

"RAF raid on Cologne last night was successful and heavy reprisals must be expected in near future. Warn all services to be on alert particularly during this moon."

JUNE 10th

Alert 00.13am to 1.23am No casualties.

16 high-explosive bombs were dropped by a single raider between 00.35am and 00.55am, falling on the South Denes, Gorleston High Street, Riverside, Burgh Road and Beccles Road. No serious damage was done although several windows were broken; several bombs also fell in the sea.

JUNE 25th

Alert midnight to 2.55am Three killed, 19 injured.

Between the hours of 1.30am and 2.50am several Dornier 217 aircraft from their base at Soesterberg,

Holland, dropped approximately 1,500 incendiary bombs from a great height, over a wide area, followed by eight high-explosive bombs.

Many large fires were started and despite great efforts by the professional and volunteer fire-fighters the parish church of St Nicholas was destroyed, only a shell remaining when daylight broke. Also destroyed was the barrel store of Lacons Brewery and Bretts Furniture Store on North Quay. Serious damage was done to Palmers warehouse and to the rear of shops in the Market Place and Howard Street and fires broke out in many other properties including Watlings maltings, Lacons Boiler House, Smith and Daniels shop in the Market Place, the Conservative Club and the Hospital School. Four houses in Northgate Street were damaged as were the Gas Works, Electricity Works and Docwras Middlegate Street Sweet Factory.

A bomb which fell at the rear of the Library caused great confusion — books and bookcases were hurled in all directions — while the fire at Lacons caused casks of spirits to explode, adding to the general noise and confusion. (Following the damage to the Library the remaining books were moved to 16 and 17 Hall Quay, formerly Clowes Grocery stores, where the library remained until rebuilt in the 1960s.)

One stick of bombs fell between Rows 107 and 128, an area already devastated by earlier raids, causing damage to the ancient remains of the Greyfriars Cloisters.

Damage in Middlegate Street, June 25th 1942.

The shell of the Parish Church of St Nicholas after the incendiary fire on June 25th 1942. Photo Great Yarmouth Library

Lacons Brewery Stores on North Quay after the rubble had been cleared away showing the full extent of the damage caused on June 25th 1942.

The Rampart Road Maltings of E Lacons & Co.   (left)

Brewery Stores, North Quay, the morning after the raid.   (below)

The burnt out interior of the Parish Church.

An eye witness to this raid was Mr Marshall who remembers, as a child, being woken by his mother, the family then living at 15 Palgrave Road. Incendiaries were burning in front gardens and in the passage at the rear of the houses and neighbours were trying to put them out with sand bags which were always kept at street corners and near lamp posts for such occasions. A friend told him that helpers were needed on one of the fire tenders on North Quay that was pumping water from the river to fight the fire at Lacons Brewery. The boys were given the job of throwing buckets of water onto the pump to stop it overheating, filling the buckets by lowering them on a rope into the river.

As the fire fighters worked they could hear the swishing sound of more incendiary bombs falling, turning over and over in the air. Above this was the drone of the enemy planes.

The boys eventually left the pump and went along the Row beside Lacons emerging opposite the parish church. They had heard that the church was on fire but were not prepared for the sight that met them. All the church windows were bright red and flames were leaping from the roof. The steeple had already fallen; flames were leaping from the tower. The boys then quickly made for home, fearing the flames would make too good a target for yet more planes.

The church had been guarded by members of the Boys Brigade, who had been on fire-watching duty for

many months. They were however completely beaten by the magnitude of the initial fire which had started between the base of the tower and the south transept. Within five minutes the church was well alight and 15 minutes later the spire collapsed. Among the very few items that could be saved were the cross and ornaments from the High Altar, the musical library and some of the vicar's robes.

The loss of the parish church was a savage blow to the town. A restoration fund was opened almost immediately and the vicar, the Rev L J Baggott, who had been inducted less than a month previously, assured the people "The parish church will rise again, of that I have no doubt."

(It was 20 years before the church was restored and rededicated, the church of St Peters serving as Parish Church for that period).

The destruction of the largest parish church in England attracted a lot of press coverage and messages of sympathy were received from many quarters including Coventry whose cathedral had suffered a similar fate earlier in the war.

JULY 4th

Alert 1.35am to 2.18am No casualties.

Two raiders took part in this raid, the first dropping flares on the marram grass to the north east of the

The Revolving Bookcase, one of the unusual item lost with the destruction of the Parish Church. Photo P Trett

The elaborately carved pulpit in St Nicholas church before the war. Photo P Trett

Lacons Joinery Shop, destroyed on June 25th 1942.

The Corporation Refuse Destructor, Tar Works Road, destroyed in the early hours of July 4th 1942.

Borough, setting it alight. As these flares fell they lit up the town and the second raider came in from the sea, to be met by searchlights and ground fire. This plane dropped one high-explosive bomb which hit the Corporation refuse destructor, on the corner of Tar Works Road and Caister Road. The buildings were reduced to a tangled mass of machinery and rubble with only the tall chimney left standing, but this was unsafe and was quickly demolished. This was a relief to many Newtown residents who were convinced that the chimney was used by enemy pilots as a landmark.

St Pauls Institute, on Caister Road almost opposite the destructor, was damaged by the blast and two buses in the Bus Station were also destroyed.

JULY 12th

Alert 1.40am to 2.25am Two killed, seven injured.

In this raid four high-explosive bombs fell in the area around the Eastern Counties Bus Station, St Peters Road. Damage was done to Marine Passage, Devonshire Road and Napoleon Place.

One bomb hit the bus station and this is where the two people were killed, a fireguard and a woman.

In all 12 buses were damaged, six nearby shops, a public house, an RAF clothing store and about 40 houses.

The German communique the following day stated:
"Last night the Luftwaffe attacked with heavy bombs important war objectives on the English East Coast."

JULY 24th

00.26am One injured.

A number of houses in the Queens Road and Havelock Road area were damaged when a single raider dropped four high-explosive bombs in the grounds of the Royal Naval Hospital. An electricity sub-station was seriously damaged, resulting in a failure of lights at the south end of the town. Windows were blown out over a considerable area and slates and tiles littered roads.

Part of the Royal Naval Barracks damaged July 24th 1942. Photo Great Yarmouth Library

JULY 29th

8.56am Two killed, 15 injured.

Two days before this raid a Dornier 217 had been shot down off Yarmouth by a Mosquito from 151 Squadron. From the same German base came another Dornier 217, taking advantage of cloud, to drop four high-explosive bombs across the residential area from Royal Avenue to Palgrave Road. Salisbury, Hamilton, Harley, Arundel and Alderson Roads all suffered damage and a house on the corner of Alderson and Palgrave Road was totally destroyed.

In this breakfast-time raid one small shop was demolished, 27 houses needed to be demolished, 38 more houses and two shops were seriously damaged and a total of 550 other houses superficially damaged.

The house and shop on the corner of Alderson and Palgrave Roads, destroyed in the breakfast time raid on July 29th 1942. Photo Great Yarmouth Library

Damaged houses in Royal Avenue, July 29th 1942.

AUGUST 22nd

Alert 10.23pm to 11.55pm Six injured.

While being pursued by a night fighter a lone raider dropped four high-explosive bombs on Middleton Road, Gorleston, at 11.35pm. One empty house was demolished in Baliol Road and the six casualties, all one family, were in a house on the opposite side of the road hit by the blast.

A Warden reported that the plane had come in very low from the west, closely followed by a fighter, and could be clearly seen in the moonlight.

The other bombs fell on a playing field and railway embankment, part of the M & GN Lowestoft line, damaging it.

Salisbury Road, July 29th 1942. Photo Great Yarmouth Library

In the early morning of December 12th two high-explosive bombs fell in the sea off Britannia Pier, causing no problems.

OCTOBER 19th

Alert 6.55am to 8.10am One injured.

There were many scattered raids in the early morning over much of East Anglia and Essex. Lowestoft guns claimed a Junkers 88 and the Norwich area was attacked. In all some 35 enemy planes took part. A Junkers 88 was shot down at Bradwell in Essex, and it was a similar plane that made the raid on Great Yarmouth at 7.16am. As it approached, sweeping low over the Breydon marshes, it machine-gunned a train steaming towards Lowestoft before releasing four 500 kg bombs on the town.

All bombs failed to explode, one falling in the river Bure near the Yacht Station, one in the garden of 4 River Road, another at the rear of 1 Burgh Road and another in the garden of 31 North River Road. The Naval Bomb Disposal Squad later safely defused all these bombs.

OCTOBER 21st

Alert 8.37pm to 9.50pm No casualties.

At 8.52pm four high-explosive bombs were dropped in the sea at the north end of the town and shortly after, at 9.05pm, six incendiary bombs and flares fell in the Southtown Road area, some near the Rumbold Arms public house and other on the marshes to the west.

DECEMBER 22nd

9.27am Eight killed, 27 injured.

A very low flying Dornier 217 dropped two high-explosive bombs in the area of Higham Place and Isaacs Buildings and between there and Albion Road ten phosphorus incendiary bombs. St Mary's School was set on fire and several small fires broke out in houses but these were quickly extinguished. These were a new type of incendiary bomb, not used in previous raids on the town.

The plane was engaged by ground defences and returned their fire with its own machine guns as it sped over the town.

Considerable damage was done in this raid and rescue work went on throughout the morning to retrieve bodies and rescue injured from the ruins of many houses.

The Report Centre log book entry for this raid reads as follows:

0945 Minor Bombing report to Cambridge.
Bombs dropped at 0927 St Nicholas Road opposite Silk Factory. Overhead cables damaged. Some casualties, number unknown.

1059 Damage Report to Regional Controller.

Two high-explosives estimated at 500 kilos and a number of 50 kilo oil and phosphorus bombs, believed 10, dropped in the centre of the town. One of the high-explosive bombs dropped on a small cottage in Higham Place about 20 houses damaged, a number of people are trapped and rescue work proceeding. The others dropped in residential district. Phosphorus bombs caused 4 small fires in dwelling houses occupied by the services. A school was damaged. One bomb broke but failed to explode, another failed to explode intact and being dealt with by naval BDS. Damage to gas, electricity and water mains, telephone cable damaged. Fairly considerable damage to Co-Operative Society Central Stores and Dairy but anticipate work can continue. Fairly widespread damage to houses and small shops in vicinity and extending to houses and small shops in Market Place. To time of reporting one person killed and 17 injured. Further casualties expected.
One Rest Centre opened. Number of people homeless and for the time being have been accommodated by friends or relatives.
1145 RHQ War Room enquired if would like to have the Electrical Detector for trapped casualties.
1215 to RHQ from Controller.

Ref. your 1140 hrs. the use of listening apparatus has been borne in mind but up to present the whereabouts of trapped known and can be heard and should apparatus be needed application will be made.

1345 Special Report to RC.

Ref. mine 1050 hrs. the approximate damage to property mostly dwelling houses is as follows: Demolished or will need to be demolished 50, seriously damaged 100, slightly damaged 600. First aid repairs have been effected. Assistance being given by NFS. Local labour is being recalled from Lowestoft and Norwich. Casualties to time of reporting 6 killed, 5 seriously injured, 20 slightly injured. So far as can be ascertained all persons have been accounted for. 45 people have been accomodated at the Rest Centre and more are expected. Everything under control. Two local canteens opened.

This entry was typical of the detailed reports made following each raid sent to the Regional Controller from where national statistics were produced enabling the whole picture of the country at war to be compiled.

It was reported that a heavy anti-aircraft battery and a light battery between them shot down a Dornier 217 as it headed out to sea on that Tuesday morning. Many member of the batteries were ATS girls and this was their first hit. This was probably the plane that had caused the damage and destruction described above.

It was the last raid of the year.

An unexploded bomb being excavated on South Quay, October 24th 1942, using a dewatering plant. Photo Great Yarmouth Library

A—SLUNG POSITION.   B—ALERT POSITION.

FIG. 11—SERVICE RESPIRATOR.

Illustrations from the ARP Practical Guide.

The air-raids continued to decline in 1943, only seven raids being recorded for the whole year. Indiscriminate bombing and machine gun attacks still caused much damage and among the 72 people killed and 124 injured were members of the WRNS and the ATS when their quarters were destroyed.

Low flying aircraft became a problem and the silver, hydrogen filled, barrage baloons were introduced over the town. Each balloon was anchored a few hundred feet above ground level by steel ropes thereby providing a hazard to the raiding aircraft.

The War Department agreed to compensate the Corporation in respect of the occupation and mining of the beaches by the military authorities. At Gorleston the equivalent to the British Restaurant in Yarmouth Market Place was opened in November at the Baptist Chapel.

JANUARY 11th

12.04pm Two injured.

A Dornier 217 based in Holland made a low level attack with cannon fire on the town. Earlier it had machine-gunned and dropped bombs on a train as it approached Yarmouth, seriously injuring a passenger. As the plane flew low over the river, close to the Police Station on Hall Quay, it was hit by gunfire from the ground defences. Part of the plane was seen to fall away and when later recovered was found to be riddled with bullet holes. As the Dornier 217 banked away from the river over Southtown it sprayed the Haven Bridge and Station Road area with petrol from a ruptured fuel tank. It then jettisoned the remainder of its bomb load in Breydon Water and with its left wing down and wobbling violently it made out to sea, where it crashed.

An AFS man, William Patterson, was hit by a splinter from a cannon shell which went through the advertisement boards in Station Road. Mrs Pearce, in her tobaconist shop on Bridge Road, had a narrow escape when a machine gun bullet shattered a glass panel in the door, passed through a postcard stand and finished up in a tobacco tin.

MARCH 18th

6.28am Nine killed, 27 injured.

A single plane, in poor weather conditions, dropped six high-explosive bombs across the southern part of the town. One fell on the engine house at Masons Laundry

The Southtown maltings of Watney, Combe & Reid. March 18th 1943.

in Queens Road, which had only just been rebuilt following an earlier raid. People sleeping in a nearby shelter had a lucky escape; the crater caused by the bomb reached the side of the shelter.

Another bomb fell in the grounds of the Naval Hospital, doing no damage except to demolish a wall and blast the fronts of houses opposite. A terrace of houses in Admiralty Road was damaged but all the houses were empty at the time. The front of St James Church was also damaged by flying debris. In Queens Road four houses were badly damaged and Melton Lodge, used as a Naval Hospital, had to be evacuated owing to an unexploded bomb.

The worst incident in this raid occured when a bomb scored a direct hit on a house at the corner of Queens Road and Nelson Road South. This house was used as a hostel for the WRNS, the girls all being asleep at the time of the raid.

Casualty services and rescue parties, aided by servicemen, dug into the ruins and by tunneling into the rubble came upon a group of five girls who were rescued unhurt. 13 girls were finally rescued from the ruins of the house but eight had died and 27 were injured. Fire broke out in the ruins but this did not deter the gallant efforts of the rescuers to reach the girls.

Later an unexploded bomb was found in the grounds of Shadingfield Lodge and another near the Wellington Pier.

The WRNS quarters at the junction of Queens Road and Nelson Road South after the raid that killed eight girls on March 18th 1943. Photo Great Yarmouth Library

MARCH 18th

11.16pm One killed, three injured.

The second raid of the day came late in the evening. A Dornier 217 based in Holland, accompanied by Junkers 88s, circled over the town for some time in the moonlight. Flares were dropped followed by two parachute mines, one on the roadway at the south end of the Fishwharf, the other falling on the Southtown Maltings of Watney Combe and Reid. The mine at the Fishwharf damaged a coal conveyor which served the power station, whilst superficial damage was done to the power station itself. Among the property damaged at Southtown was the Half Way House public house.

Two more mines were dropped west of Caister Road, the blast damaging the factory of Smith's Crisps and nearby houses.

Earlier in the evening, at 10.30pm, approximately 240 incendiary bombs were dropped on the South Denes and Gorleston High Street. Stead and Simpsons shoe shop caught fire but this, and other smaller fires, were soon dealt with by the NFS and firewatchers.

The German communique, issued after this raid, claimed that the Luftwaffe had attacked the industrial town of Norwich and the harbour of Great Yarmouth. It declared that large fires were seen burning when the planes turned for home and stated that three planes were missing.

MARCH 28th

9.45pm to 11pm No casualties.

There was considerable air activity and gunfire as a force of Dornier 217s crossed the East Anglian coast, apparently attempting to reach Norwich. The heavy barrage of anti-aircraft gunfire and the efforts of Mosquito fighter planes from 68 Squadron turned back the raiders.

At 10.15pm a Dornier 217 from Holland dropped four Fire-pot incendiary bombs in the area of Crow Hall Farm and Bendish Avenue, Gorleston but no damage or casualties were reported.

MAY 7th

7.11am 13 killed, 51 injured.

This raid marked the first appearance of the FW 190 Fighter Bomber over the town. The Luftwaffe introduced these planes in lieu of fast strategic bombers and the pilots were trained to fly so low as to come in under the radar screen and bomb specific targets, such as gasometers.

A post-war view of the site of Burroughs Wine Store, on the corner of Church Plain. The building was destroyed on May 7th 1943 and in 1959 the present Gallon Pot public house was built on the site.

The FW 190 was armed with a 20mm cannon and was fitted with drop tanks to increase its range. A 1000 kg bomb was carried under the fuselage.

Soon after first light 20 of these planes made landfall higher up the coast and fanned out from the north west over the town. 19 bombs were dropped indiscriminately. One failed to explode and landed at Southtown Station, between the lines and the platform. A Naval Bomb Disposal officer, who was waiting for a train, immediately defused the bomb and rendered it safe.

Another bomb exploded outside Vauxhall Railway Station, having bounced off the lines and passed through two coaches before exploding in the forecourt. A lorry was set on fire and a coffee stall demolished. The owner of the stall, Mrs Wright, was killed, as were two men in the lorry.

As the planes roared in from the west several places were hit, including Lichfield, Anson, Albany, Wolseley,

The old George and Dragon public house on Church Plain became the office for Burroughs wine business after the bombing of 1943.

Southtown, Olive, Winifred and Mill Roads, South Market Road and Melville Terrace on Regent Road. The Fishermen's Hospital and the Priory School were damaged by blast. In the Market Place Burroughs Wine Store on the corner of Brewery Plain was destroyed by a direct hit and another bomb plunged through the roof of the Northgate School First Aid Post.

The widespread damage and large casualty list testified to the efficiency of the FW 190 raid. The speed of the raid, the little warning received and the psychological effect of the roaring engines brought a new element into the air raids. A firewatcher on the Regal cinema said "I saw the planes sweep in, one after another, firing their cannons at the street and releasing their bombs which seemed to glide away and almost travel like aeroplanes themselves over the roofs until they hit and exploded. It was without doubt the fastest raid we have had."

In total 105 houses were seriously damaged, 1100 slightly damaged, 13 people killed, eight seriously injured and 43 slightly injured in this raid.

MAY 11th

8.45am 49 killed, 41 injured.

Four days later a further 20 FW 190s swept in very low out of an early morning sea mist and against a rising sun. Two planes were destroyed, one by an intercepting Mustang fighter, the other by anti-aircraft gunners and several more were damaged. The remainder, machine-gunning as they went, dropped 14 high-explosive bombs at scattered points in the residential area at the north end of the town. The enemy planes came in so quickly there was no time to sound the alert. Only a Crash Warning sounded as the first bomb fell at 8.45am.

The planes roared over North Drive just five minutes after a squad of 30 ATS girls had marched down the road and entered their billets at Whitfield House, next to the Imperial Hotel on the corner of Sandown Road. Bombs from one of the planes hit the building and within seconds it was a mass of smoking rubble, the girls inside. One of the rescue squad, Mr Dean, later described the scene. "I heard the roar of the planes and right in front of me a crashing sound. Then there was another, and I saw the building burst apart just as five enemy planes came screaming overhead. The blast lifted me off the motor roller I was driving. The planes were so low that I could see the black crosses on them, they seemed to lift themselves up to clear the rooftops. When I looked towards the billet I saw the awful wreckage."

Soldiers and rescue squads worked for many hours to recover bodies from the wreckage. A total of 26 girls were killed. They were later buried at Caister with full military honours.

Other bombs fell on Caister Road, Beatty Road, Seymour Avenue, North Denes, and Sandown,

Hamilton and Jellicoe Roads. A victim of the machine-gunning was Mrs Riches who died after her car was shot up as she drove along. There were many eye-witnesses to this raid. A teacher cycling to school said "I flung myself into the gutter but each time I tried to get up another plane seemed to roar just above my head." A ten-year-old boy saw one of the planes just over the rooftops, "I saw a bomb leave one of the planes and it fell at the back of some houses not far from me. The next thing I knew was that I was covered with feathers from chickens that must have been killed in one of the gardens."

Another bomb fell on a row of houses opposite a Nursing Home and mothers were cut by flying glass, while yet another bomb demolished a small shopping centre when it fell in the middle of the row of shops. This started a fire which had to be dealt with by the NFS.

An official narrative from Coltishall read:

"A few hours after dawn 20 190s attacked Yarmouth. They were engaged by 4 Mustangs of 613 Squadron on their way to recce shipping off the Dutch coast. F/O Townsend got one and another was damaged some two miles out."

The total casualties for this raid were 49 dead and 41 injured; the total for the two FW 190 raids were 62 dead and 92 injured. It is fortunate that this proved to be the last raid of this type on the town, although a further one was planned for July 6th. The timely intervention of four Typhoons of 56 Squadron drove the attacking FW 190s off before they reached the town. Following the May attacks a balloon barrage was installed over the town as a deterrent to low level attacks of this kind.

OCTOBER 23rd

Alert 10.59pm to 11.52pm No casualties.

Flares preceded this Saturday night raid when at

Eighteenth century buildings in Row 118 damaged beyond repair. Photographed in 1943 prior to demolition.

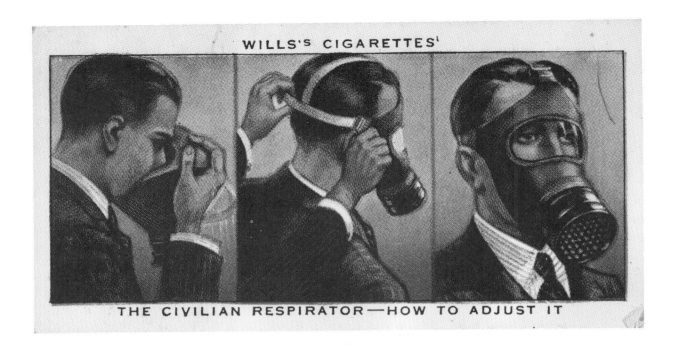

WILLS'S CIGARETTES

THE CIVILIAN RESPIRATOR—HOW TO ADJUST IT

More cards from the Will's cigarettes selection.

11.30pm about 240 incendiary bombs were dropped on open ground behind School Lane, Gorleston and Ferryside. Searchlights caught the raiders in their beams but despite heavy ground fire the planes escaped damage.

Country-wide air raids were greatly reduced in 1944. Evacuees returned to Yarmouth and war damaged property repairs began. New housing estates were planned and the Magdalen College Estate at Gorleston was considered for 2000 houses, 300 to be built by private enterprise. The Council bought the required 178 acres of land at a market value of £18,800.

Four acres of land were bought to the west of Gorleston Cemetery and allocated for the erection of factory-built 'pre-fab' houses.(This later became known as the Shrublands Estate).

With thoughts of a holiday season the Publicity Committee was reformed and amended the 5000 copies of the guide they still had in stock.

Temporary repairs were made to the Jetty in September and it was reopened for anglers only. Some of the 'defence works' were dismantled along the Parade and discussions began on clearing the beaches of mines.

JUNE 1st

1944 3.20am No casualties.

Four high-explosive bombs were dropped harmlessly on the foreshore at the South Denes by an Me 410. This proved to be the last air-raid on the town.

Although the country was still on a state of alert until 1945 the threat of invasion had passed and some defences were relaxed.

The Home Guard stood down on 3rd December 1944, the final orders being given at an assembly held at the Royal Aquarium, attended by 90 officers and 1,849 other ranks of the 11th (Norfolk) Battalion Home Guard.

The last warning was sounded on the sirens at 1.23pm on April 30th 1945. On May 8th 1945 hostilities in Europe came to an end and the threat to the coastal towns of East Anglia was lifted.

The total number of Alerts sounded from September 1939 to April 1945 was 2046.

The town began its post-war recovery and programmes for rebuilding damaged houses, rebuilding and re-equipping factories and repair to fishing premises were started.

The Publicity Committee approved a limited programme of summer attractions for 1945 with a ten week season at the Wellington Pier Pavilion, the Marina and the Winter Gardens. At the Wellington Pier Pavilion 'Showtime' opened on June 30th and played to packed houses until September 8th, while in the Winter Gardens 'Harry Roy's Tiger Ragamuffins' played for dancing twice daily, at 3pm and 8pm.

The military authorities began the arduous task of clearing the mines from the beaches and the central area was cleared by the end of June, opening again to the public at 5pm on Friday July 13th, although the Council decided there would be no deckchair, boat or tent hire concessions for that summer. There were no attractions north of the Britannia Pier and the Pier itself remained closed, as did the Jetty and the Pleasure Beach. The Britannia Pier finally reopened in July 1946.

The story of the town's recovery in the post war years is not within the scope of this book and therefore we end this account of the town at war in 1945.

The war finally ended with the surrender of Japan on September 2nd 1945.

Saving Fuel in the KITCHEN

Keep pots, pans and stoves clean—this saves fuel.

Make use of every bit of oven space when baking. Soups and many vegetables can be cooked in the oven as well as joints, potatoes and puddings. If there is any space left, cook extra dishes which can be eaten cold the next day.

When you are not using your oven, a steamer is a great saving as you can cook a complete meal in it. If you don't possess a steamer, try using a colander with an ordinary pan. Fish can be steamed between two soup plates over a pan of hot water.

If you are cooking on a gas burner, never let the flames leap up the sides of the kettle or pan. Use a small burner in preference to a large one unless you are in a hurry.

Minutes mean money where fuel is concerned, so don't get the kettle boiling until you are ready to make the tea.

Also don't absent-mindedly fill the kettle when you only need half that amount of boiling water!

Serve as many salad meals as you can. Salad, cheese, brown bread and butter or margarine, milk and fruit make a real health dinner for both adults and children. A meal like this uses no fuel.

OUR FOOD · OUR DEFENCE

THE line of Food Defence runs through all our homes. It is where we must be always on our guard. The watchword is careful housekeeping.

It may seem so simple, this urgent duty, that we may tend to overlook its full meaning. A little saving here and there—how can that really help us to win the war? A little here and there, with our 45 million people all contributing, becomes an immense amount. Take one example. Many people make tea by allowing one teaspoonful a head, and an additional teaspoonful "for the pot." The teaspoonful "for the pot." is unnecessary. It is equal over the whole population to sixty shiploads a year. We must have those ships to bring munitions.

Remember how much of our food comes from overseas—more than 20 million tons in a peace-time year. Let us picture the convoys, bringing the cargoes to our shores and let us be very careful.

As a companion to this leaflet the Ministry of Food have issued a leaflet called "How to eat wisely in War-time." It deals with the effect of food on health. It sets out the foods in four groups, according to the nourishment which they supply, and shows housewives the variety from which they can make their choice.

Further leaflets will be issued on the ways of using particular foods.

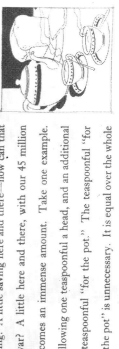

GROUP 1.	BODY-BUILDING FOODS
	They build the body and prevent the tissues wearing out.

MILK · CHEESE · EGGS · MEAT', FISH

★ Many vegetable foods, such as peas and beans, bread and potatoes, help in body-building; but they are not such good body-builders as these five.

GROUP 2.	ENERGY FOODS
	They provide fuel for the human body.

BACON & HAM · BREAD · BUTTER or MARGARINE · CHEESE · DRIED FRUIT · DRIPPING, SUET & LARD · HONEY · OATMEAL · POTATOES · RICE · TAPIOCA, SAGO · SUGAR

GROUP 3.	PROTECTIVE FOODS
	They protect us from disease.

MILK · BUTTER or MARGARINE · CHEESE · EGGS · HERRINGS · SALMON (tinned or fresh) LIVER

GROUP 4.	

POTATOES · GREEN VEGETABLES & SALADS · FRUIT (fresh or tinned but not dried) CARROTS · TOMATOES · WHOLEMEAL BREAD

Protective Foods are needed if we are to be properly nourished. They build the teeth and bones and help us to resist infection.

041014

Careful Buying and Careful Cookery from 'Wise Housekeeping in War-time'

A post-war aerial view of the town centre showing the large area of Middlegate that was destroyed, mainly in 1941. Photo Memory Lane Studio

APPENDIX

THE STRENGTH OF THE ARP RESCUE SERVICE IN 1939.

9   Ambulance Stations with 3 vehicles each.
10 Cars.
4   Decontamination Squads.
5   Light Rescue Squads.
1   Heavy Rescue Squad.
4   'First Aid Posts each with 15 personnel.

FIRST AID POSTS.

Northgate School, Garrison Road.
St James School, Admiralty Road.
Edward Worlledge School, Lichfield Road.
Stradbroke School, Lowestoft Road.

FIRST-AID PARTY DEPOTS.

St Paul's Institute, Hamilton Road.
North Mission, Northgate Street.
St George's Hall, King Street.
Greenacre School, Dickens Avenue.
Cobholm JTC, Critten's Road.
St Andrew's Hall, School Lane Gorleston.

AMBULANCE STATIONS.

Morris's Garage, Sandringham Avenue.
King's Garage, North Quay.
St John's Garage, Regent Road.
Nelson Garage, Southgates Road.
Toby's Garage, Main Cross Road.
Long's Garage, Beccles Road.
Hayman's Garage, Lowestoft Road.
Watson's Garage, Southtown Road.

FEEDING AND REST CENTRES.

Deneside Central Hall, Young Peoples Department.
Children's Home, Addison Road.
St Luke's Mission, Mill Road, Cobholm.

SLEEPING CENTRES.

Caister Road Methodist Church.
St Paul's Institute, Estcourt Road.
North Mission, Northgate Street.
Congregational Church, Middlegate Street.
Methodist Mission, Queens Road.
Methodist Hall, Cobholm.
Methodist Church, Beccles Road, Gorleston.
Methodist Church, Nile Road, Gorleston.
Congregational Church, High Street, Gorleston.

BIBLIOGRAPHY

The main source of information for **this book**, additional to those mentioned in the **introduction**, has been a collection of cutting from newspapers of various dates between 1940 and 1944. These newspapers include:

Yarmouth Mercury.
Eastern Evening News.
Eastern Daily Press.

Other information has been taken from:

Great Yarmouth Front Line Town, Charles Box, 1945.
Front Line, 1940−1941, London Stationery Office, 1942.
The Defence of the United Kingdom, Collier.
Fortifications of East Anglia, P Kent, 1988.
Transport in Great Yarmouth, Volume 3, T Barker, 1988.

Documents from the Norfolk and Norwich Record Office:

Report Centre Log Books, 6 Volumes, 1939−1945.
Wardens' Report Sheets, 96 Bundles, 1940−1944.
Detailed maps of bomb strikes.

INDEX

This select index includes street names, organisations, major buildings and businesses in the main text. It does not cover lists within the main text, or the appendices.

Lacons Brewery   51 52 53 54
Lady Haven Road   36
Lancaster Road   45
Lawn Avenue   33
Library   51
Lichfield Road   49 62
Local Defence Volunteers   10
Lowestoft Road, Gorleston   36
38
42
Luftwaffe   7 11 12 18 19 26 31
32 62

Manby Road   24
Manual School   27
Marine Crescent   18
Marine Parade   17 18 19 20 27
28 45 50
Marine Passage   55
Market Gates   24
Market Place   21 22 31 48 51
58 60 63
Maygrove   24
Micawber Avenue   46
Middle Market Road   19 22 23
Middle Road West   26
Middlegate Street   22 32 35 42
51 66
Middleton Road, Gorleston   38
40
56
Mill Road   36 42 63
Mission Road, Cobholm   34

Napoleon Place   55
National Fire Service   10 62 63
Naval Barracks   20 21
Nelson Gardens   15 17 45 50
Nelson Road Central   33
Nelson Road North   26 27
Nelson Road, Gorleston   15 36
Nelson Road South   61
Nelson's Monument   17
Nettle Hill East   19
Newcastle Road   26 46
Newtown   31 48 55
Nile Road, Gorleston   33
Norfolk Square   33
North Battery   7
North Denes   45 63
North Drive   7 18 19 33 43 46
49 63
North Market Road   23
North Quay   33 51 52 53
North River Road   57
Northgate Street   24 29 31 33
37 42 49 51
Nurses' Home   38

Old White Lion Public House   27
Olive Road   63
Ordnance Road   26
Ormond Road   24

Palace Cinema, Gorleston   34
Palgrave Road   24 29 33 53 56
Parachute Mine   12
Parish Church   51 52 53 54
Phosphorus Incendiary   12
Pier Walk, Gorleston   16
Pleasure Beach   17 20 50 64

Queen Street   22
Queen's Place   25
Queen's Road   15 32 46 55 61

Racecourse   31 40
RAF Coltishall   12 15 16 46 50
63
Raleigh Avenue   46
Rampart Road   49 52
Regal Cinema   24 33 63
Regent Road   11 19 25 33 63
Regent Street   49
Report Centre   8 15 22 24 31
32 33 42 57
Revolving Tower   21
Reynolds Garage   27 28
River Road   57
Rodney Road   27 28
Rows, The   7 22 31 32 33 42
51 53 63
Royal Aquarium   18 33 64
Royal Avenue   56
Royal Naval Hospital   15 17 18
19 20 27
55
Royal Naval Training School   25
Rumbold Arms Public House   29
42
57
Runham Vauxhall   29 31

St George's Park   37
St Luke's Terrace   42
St Nicholas Road   26 57
St Peter's Plain   27 42
St Peter's Road   45 55
Salisbury Road   18 28 33 45 46
56 57
Sandown Road   18 63
Sandringham Avenue   46
School Lane, Gorleston   34 64
Sefton Lane   42
Seymour Avenue   63
Smith's Crisp Factory   40 61
South Beach Parade   45
South Denes   22 24 42 45 46
50 62 64

South Market Road   33 63
South Pier   7
South Quay   22 31 33 42 46 58
Southgates Road   25 26 42 46
Southtown   13 15 16 22 24 33
34 36 43 48 60 61
Southtown Road   29 32 35 40
42 46 57 63
Southtown Station   42 62
Springfield Road, Gorleston   33
Stafford Road   36
Station Road   60
Steam Mill Lane   36
Stone Cutter's Quay   7
Suffling Road   42
Suffolk Road   24

Tar Works Road   55
Tavern Lane, Gorleston   22
Tennyson Road   43 46
Theatre Plain   24 48
Town Hall   27 34
Trafalgar Road   8
Tramway Hotel, Gorleston   38

Union Road   19
Upper Cliff Road, Gorleston   16
33

Vauxhall Railway Station   13 62

Walpole Road   20
Wardens   8 10 13 21 25 28 31
33 40
Waterways   18
Wellington Pier   7 18 61 64
Wellington Place   37
Western Road, Gorleston   38
Winifred Road   63
Wolseley Road   15 62
Wood Farm Lane, Gorleston   46

Yareside Works   16
York Road   27 45